25
REASONS
WHY
JESUS
WAS
BORN

25
REASONS
WHY
JESUS
WAS
BORN

Daily Reflections for Celebrating Advent

SCOTT JACKSON

 Blessed Light Press

25 Reasons Why Jesus Was Born:
Daily Reflections for Celebrating Advent

©2020 by Gregory Scott Jackson

scottinargentina@gmail.com

ISBN: 978-1-7348965-0-3 (softcover)
ISBN: 978-1-7348965-1-0 (ebook)
Library of Congress Control Number: 2020906614

Cover Design: Erik M. Peterson
Interior Design: Katherine Lloyd, The DESK

To the students of Seminario Bíblico William Carey in Córdoba, Argentina. Your hard work, dedication, and sacrifices made in order to advance the gospel in Latin America are truly remarkable. You are my heroes in the faith.

CONTENTS

PREFACE

A tension simmers within my heart throughout every Christmas season. The holy, pious side of me wants to focus on the reason for the season, but there is a physical reality which often distracts my soul away from just how awesome the miraculous birth of Christ was and is. If you are at all like me, by about December 27th or so, you plan to "take it easier" next year on all the hustle and bustle of gifts, decorations, year-end parties, and all the other "superficial" things that detract from the real meaning of Christmas. Yet when the next year rolls around, we still struggle with all the stress and with keeping our hearts and minds focused on the important things.

Don't get me wrong: I am not saying that ornate decorations, parties, gifts (or the gift wrapping itself) are evil. In fact, I think they can actually be good. Carrying out traditions with others during a certain event or festival is what often makes it so special. This has been true since the beginning of mankind. God himself even prompted the Israelites in the days of old to celebrate important religious holidays with certain meals, music, activities and rituals.

I guess my problem with Christmas as I've known it boils down to priorities. Will the activities and rituals take over so that I forget the reason I'm carrying out those activities? Entering any mall between Black Friday and Christmas Eve can certainly be a test for where my heart is during the holiday season. Just hearing others fight, worry, or complain over buying some gift can lead my heart off course: suddenly I too am fretting about my gift list rather than marveling at the incarnate Savior who is the only gift I need. Our world invents plenty of distractions, but ultimately, it is not something outside of us that determines whether we truly celebrate Christmas for what it means. God, as we know, is far more concerned with what is going on inside of our hearts than all of the circumstances that surround us.

One year, during Advent, I was feeling especially distracted and upset about the Christmas season. I felt more like a bah-humbug than a simple shepherd coming to worship the Lord Jesus. In order to get my mind and heart on the right course, I began to set time aside to ponder about the meaning of Christmas. I asked myself: What is Christmas about? Why did Jesus come to earth as a baby human being? This book is a product of my time reflecting on these questions. These 25 daily readings are designed to be read from December 1st through December 25th, but they can be read during any period of the year. Whenever you read these, I ask you to spend more than the few minutes each chapter requires. Take the time to reflect personally on that particular reason why Jesus was born, and seek God in prayer.

My hope and desire is that you come to appreciate the incarnation of Jesus, that you understand more about the reason he came, and that by doing so you would ultimately praise him and give him all the glory that he deserves.

Reason #1

TO BE THE LAST SACRIFICE

One of the main themes that spans the whole Bible is the very real, physical presence of God on the earth. How can a perfect, all-powerful being relate to and dwell among finite, imperfect beings? The answer to that question is given to us in the entire story of the Bible. It is of great comfort to know that our God is good and wants to be with us. He knows that mankind definitely benefits from being in a right relationship with him. As he nears his people on earth, they come to know him and understand their purpose in life, along with many other blessings.

In the Old Testament, before Jesus was born, God chose to dwell specifically among the Israelites. Foreigners who wanted to belong to God's people were also allowed into the community. Enjoying fellowship with God's people meant experiencing the benefits of living in God's presence. God provided guidance, protection from enemies, and even food on some occasions. This is why the greatest punishment for committing a sin was to be exiled from the community. Indeed, when one of God's laws was disobeyed, the person who was guilty was separated from

fellowship with other Israelites, and even worse, they were isolated from the very presence of God. That was a tough pill to
swallow.

Here is where sacrifices come into play. People could offer
sacrifices—by killing an animal—to show that they understood
their guilt before God and that they trusted him. God would
then allow them back into full fellowship within the community. Scholars Raymond Dillard and Tremper Longman explain
the situation well:

> God is holy and cannot tolerate the presence of sin and
> uncleanness. Sacrifice is a way of making the unholy
> pure again and restoring fellowship in the presence of
> God. It allows the unclean who have been forced from
> the presence of God to return once again to the camp
> that is the realm of the holy.[1]

The tabernacle (which was eventually replaced by the temple) held special significance for God's people because that was
the specific place where God's presence was. Within the tabernacle and temple were all kinds of specific furnishings used
for various religious ceremonies. They served as symbols and
instruments for carrying out the relationship between God and
his people. Perhaps the most important piece of furniture was
the altar. There, a holy God met with those "dirtied" by sin and
disobedience. The altar was a place of constant movement and
activity as sinners came to present their sacrifices to God.

But these sacrifices were not perfect. They could not fully do
away with sin, so people needed to offer them again and again.
They also required priests to carry out the sacrifice, who acted
as mediators between God and the people. A person would
bring their offering to the temple and explain to the priest the

reason they were bringing it. Mostly the sacrifices were brought because they were guilty of sin, but sometimes offerings were given as a way of showing thanks. At any rate, the sacrificial system served a purpose for a time, but it all foreshadowed a greater and perfect sacrifice—that of Jesus Christ himself. Consider the following passages:

"Christ loved us and gave himself up for us as a fragrant offering and sacrifice to God" (Ephesians 5:2).

"But he has appeared once for all at the culmination of the ages to do away with sin by the sacrifice of himself" (Hebrews 9:26).

"For by one sacrifice he has made perfect forever those who are being made holy" (Hebrews 10:14).

"And where these have been forgiven, sacrifice for sin is no longer necessary" (Hebrews 10:18).

These verses show us that Jesus *willingly* gave himself up as a sacrifice to God because of our guilt. They also indicate that because Jesus was a perfect sacrifice, we no longer need the temporary sacrificial system of offering up animals for our sin. After Jesus died, both Jews and non-Jews who understood that Jesus sacrificed himself because of their own guilt did not continue the ritual of sacrificing animals on an altar because they knew that nothing other than the sacrifice of Jesus was needed.

How great a sacrifice we have in Jesus! Through faith in him, we can be fully pardoned for all our guilt! We, like the Israelites of old, can fully enjoy God's presence dwelling among us when we acknowledge our wrongs and accept the fact that he sacrificed himself in our place!

Questions to Consider

- Why was it necessary for Jesus to come as a sacrifice?
- Have I admitted that I need Jesus in order to fellowship with God?

For Further Reading

Hebrews, chapters 10–11

Reason #2

TO LIVE OUT THE LAW PERFECTLY

In yesterday's reading we saw that Jesus came to be the last sacrifice. We learned that Jesus' sacrifice was the last because it could truly take away people's sins. We should ask how did Jesus' death accomplish this? The simple answer is that God demanded a perfect sacrifice. Since all of the animals were not perfect, they could not truly appease God's wrath and thus lacked in their effectiveness. Jesus, on the other hand, was the perfect sacrifice. By *perfect* we mean without sin. Not once did Jesus disobey God.

John Piper asks, "Is the death of Jesus sufficient to cleanse us from all our sins?"[2] His answer: "Yes, but only *as the climax of a sinless life.*" His point is that it was not enough for just anyone to die on a cross, for the person who died would have had to live a perfect life. Well, the quality of perfection as a requirement disqualifies all human beings except Jesus. Only Jesus could offer the perfect sacrifice for mankind. Note the following two passages:

> "For as by the one man's disobedience the many were made sinners, so by the one man's obedience the many will be made righteous" (Romans 5:19, ESV).

"For we do not have a high priest who is unable to empathize with our weaknesses, but we have one who has been tempted in every way, just as we are—*yet he did not sin*" (Hebrews 4:15, emphasis added).

In theological terms, we describe what Jesus accomplished for us as "imputed righteousness." In everyday words, this means that when we trust Jesus as the sacrifice for our sin, his perfect, sinless, and completely righteous life is credited toward us.

Perhaps an analogy will help you understand this concept. Imagine you are in grade school and it is lunch time and you are eating with your friends. You are all very thirsty, having played a game of soccer in P.E. class just before. You pull out your bottle of water and all of your friends' faces show signs of disgust. "Ew! What happened to your water?" says one of the kids. You look at the water and something does not look right. Next, you open the bottle and the smell definitely convinces you, in spite of your thirst, that this water will in no way be going down your throat. There is nothing in your power that you can do to solve the problem, the bottle itself is too dirty to consider throwing out the water and filling it back up with water from the school fountain. The solution comes from your friend sitting to your right: "I've got an extra bottle of clean water, here you go, have mine!" Even though the clean water belonged to your friend, it became yours and you were able to enjoy it fully. This is a little bit like how it is when we receive Jesus' purity, except it cost him a lot more. In order for us to us to be restored and seen as clean in God's eyes, Jesus had to suffer and die.

In conclusion, if you are a believer in Jesus Christ—one who accepts his sacrifice on your behalf—then God, in spite of all the wrongs you have committed, sees you and declares you 100% holy, clean, and without blemish! That is a reason to celebrate the season of Christmas!

Questions to Consider

- Do you believe Jesus lived a perfect life? Why or why not?
- Does God see you as perfect? Why or why not? If you feel that you want to trust in Jesus, yet cannot understand how God can erase all of your blemishes, I encourage you to talk to a Christian friend or pastor about how you may be freed from the guilt of sin.

For Further Reading

Romans 3

Reason #3

TO ESTABLISH
A NEW COVENANT

Pretty much all of us can say that in our homes we have things on display that are special to us. Many of these things highlight certain points of our lives. A family portrait captures a moment in time we are thankful for and proud of. First day of school pictures remind us of what we were like and of our progress and growth. We display not just pictures but other things as well. Perhaps you have a diploma or certificate showing that you accomplished a specific goal, the culmination of a time of preparation and hard work. Or maybe a map showing the places you have either lived or visited. Or if not a map maybe you have something like a seashell or a ceramic work of art from a specific trip that marked your life. This list of possibilities goes on and on, but I am sure if you look around your house or someone else's place you will see things on display which mark special memories or specific moments in time, things which are treasures to their own personal story.

Now we know for sure that our lives are much more than a few special highlights. The details and specifics of our life stories are immeasurable and unfold on a day-to-day basis. In order to really get to know someone we need to do more than just look at their wedding album or souvenir collection. Yet at the same time, the milestones are there for a reason.

God has been interacting with mankind and his creation for thousands of years. The Bible tells us many details about who God is and how he has been present with us and guiding both his and our stories. There are several points along the way that serve as special highlights, events that stand out as extra important. Much like our family portraits mark important times in our lives, there are certain passages in the Bible that mark an important point at which God interacted with us. These moments in time are called covenants. Covenant is a fancy word for a treaty or formal agreement—like two business partners or countries entering a binding relationship. The treaty or written agreement explains the details of the agreement, the responsibilities each party has, and the consequences for breaking the agreement.

The various covenants God has made with humans are important because they have major short-term and long-term implications. God uses covenants to reveal his character and accomplish his plan and mission. They provide instructions about how one can relate to God and enjoy his presence. Although each covenant has been established out of God's initiative and grace, each one requires different degrees of human obedience. The covenants that stipulated specific things that people had to do in order to keep their end of the bargain have been called "conditional covenants." On the other hand, others which require no human response and rest fully on God's sovereignty have been deemed "unconditional covenants."

The covenants we see in the Old Testament are special passages of Scripture and serve as milestones marking important points in history. Here is a brief summary of the covenants before Jesus was born:

The Adamic (or sometimes called Edenic) Covenant: God promised Adam and Eve and all their future offspring eternal life in a place of paradise. The only condition was that they were to abstain from eating the fruit of the tree of the knowledge of good evil. They did not fulfill their part of the covenant and thus they suffered the consequences along with all of their offspring.

The Noahic Covenant: God promised all creatures of the earth that he will never again destroy the earth by flood.

The Abrahamic Covenant: God promised Abraham a large number of descendants and to provide a specific land for them to live in. He also promised to use Abraham's family to bless all the other nations. Abraham was called to respond by leaving his native land and travelling to the area we know today as Israel. So, in this covenant we see that God was going to do something special for a specific group of people (the Israelites), but his full intentions were to bless all the nations of the earth.

The Mosaic Covenant: God promised to provide a number of things to the Israelites such as a land to live in, abundant food to eat, peace with other nations, health, and general welfare. The Israelites were told they must not worship other gods; if they maintained their allegiance to God, the Israelites could count on God to provide for them, but if they failed, God would not guarantee continued provisions. To sum up this covenant, we may say that God is concerned about how his people live their lives and deserves to be honored with obedience.

The Davidic Covenant: About 1,000 years before Jesus was born, King David wanted to build a "house" or a temple for God. Although God was surely pleased with David's intentions, he had a surprise twist for David regarding this construction project. God revealed that he was going to build an everlasting "house" for David, promising him that from one of his descendants would come a King whose rule would never end.

If you are reading this book and are not so familiar with these covenants and perhaps are even a little confused by them, don't worry. All of them pointed toward what we call the New Covenant, which is God's promise to us through Jesus. People were expecting this covenant a long time before Jesus was born. Indeed, the New Covenant is the best one, and it was finally made possible for us through Jesus.

Months prior to the release of a movie, the producers put out "trailers" which gives people a small taste of what's to come. We then wait expectantly for that final version. God did something similar to this with the covenant that was going to be established through Jesus. Long before he established the New Covenant, he sent out messengers called prophets to speak about another covenant that would come. The "trailers" revealed that through the New Covenant, people would have the opportunity to have all their sins forgiven, know God in a personal way, have totally transformed hearts, and be filled with God's Spirit. These were huge blessings indeed, and caused many people to be waiting and expecting for God to reveal this New Covenant.

This New Covenant accomplishes amazing things, but the best part of it is that it is freely open to any living person. All of God's covenants show his grace, but the New Covenant is the crown jewel. Here is God's grace on full display, "grace upon grace" (John 1:16). It should not surprise us when Hebrews 8 makes it clear that the New Covenant established by Jesus is superior to all those previously established.

In a nutshell, the New Covenant that God has made is this: all men and women may have a right relationship with God and experience the blessedness of his presence because of Christ's sacrifice on the cross. Humans are required to do exactly zero effort in order to participate in the New Covenant. No rules, no dress code to enter God's party. As he is our King, we want to honor and obey him with our lives, that is a natural response when we are in awe of what he has done for us. But there is no pre-required checklist of things that we need to do first in order for God to accept us. Simply by trusting in Christ (and God even grants us our faith), we may enter into his New Covenant with him.

Questions to Consider

- Does everyone experience the full blessings of the New Covenant? Why or why not?
- How do you know if you have entered into this New Covenant with God?
- Why is the New Covenant superior than the others?
- Why did God go to the trouble of establishing so many other covenants before finally establishing the New Covenant? Why didn't he just start with Jesus?

For Further Reading

Hebrews 8-9

Reason #4

TO SERVE
OTHERS

We all know something about service. Don't you notice right away when you are given good service or bad service in a restaurant? Almost all businesses have something about customer service in their vision or mission statement. If someone is looking to help others in need, it is not hard to find "service projects" in the community. Maybe you have noticed others who seem particularly good at serving others, and you've tried to watch them and become more like them.

Praise God if you have someone like that in your life whom you can imitate! But know this: without Christ, we would be left in the dark regarding true servanthood. Jesus did not participate in a few service projects here and there. No, he lived a life of serving others. Servanthood was his lifestyle, not a button to be switched off and on. He could do this not merely because he was God incarnate, but also because servanthood defined, at least in part, his very existence and purpose.

In Matthew 20:28 we hear Jesus say that "the Son of Man did not come to be served but to serve, and to give his life as a ransom for many." When Christ lived on earth, part of his mission was to serve. He did not serve from time to time, for service flowed out of his very nature. Furthermore, he served both mankind and his heavenly Father: "The God of Abraham, Isaac, and Jacob, the God of our forefathers, has glorified *his servant* Jesus" (Acts 3:13, emphasis added).

Paul explains that Christ was the supreme example of a servant, and that is why he is exalted above all names:

> In your relationships with one another, have the same mindset as Christ Jesus:
>   Who, being in very nature God,
>   did not consider equality with God something to be
> used to his own advantage;
> rather, he made himself nothing
>   by taking the very nature of a servant,
>   being made in human likeness.
> And being found in appearance as a man,
>   he humbled himself
>   by becoming obedient to death—
>   even death on a cross!
>   Therefore God exalted him to the highest place
>   and gave him the name that is above every name,
> that at the name of Jesus every knee should bow,
>   in heaven and on earth and under the earth,
> and every tongue acknowledge that Jesus Christ is Lord,
>   to the glory of God the Father. (Philippians 2:5-11)

Paul's introduction to those verses suggests that those who claim the name "Christian" should necessarily be the best servants on earth as they follow and imitate Jesus. After all, serving involves releasing control of yourself and your own desires to something or someone else. If we serve God, then we let him determine the decisions we make. If we serve something else, such as money or fame, then we let those things control our affections and actions. Indeed, it is impossible to serve God if our own comforts and status are more important than making God's name famous (Luke 16:13). Consider these other statements describing Christians as servants:

- ◆ We are to use everything with which God has blessed us to serve others (1 Peter 4:10).
- ◆ We should be eager to serve (Romans 12:9-12)
- ◆ We are to serve wholeheartedly (Ephesians 6:7).
- ◆ Serving others flows from our love for them (Galatians 5:13).

Those who do great things for Christ understand these things so deeply that they define themselves as servants. Paul, who perhaps did more for the cause of spreading Christianity than anyone else, often called himself a "servant of Christ" (see, for example, the first verses of his letters to the Romans, the Philippians, and Titus).

But what about the rest of us? Service does not come easy to everyone, nor is "servant" a title that most would want to embrace. Perhaps you think serving God seems awkward or painful—at best, a never-ending list of chores to do. That makes sense if you think of God as a policeman looking to hand out tickets. Plenty of others have felt this way about God. For example, the great Martin Luther went almost mad trying to serve a God who he thought was out to get him. Eventually, he came to see God for his abundance of grace and love, and thus his service to God became joy rather than duty. This Christmas season, are you also open to changing your understanding of Jesus and what he wants for you?

The beauty of serving God is that doing so brings glory to his name *and* benefits us. The individuals I think of as great servants of God are also the ones who seem most at peace and most joyful. Like Jesus, they truly love serving their heavenly Father. I hope you see as well that our great God is indeed worthy to be served.

Questions to Consider

- How would you rate your service to others? Do you think of it as duty or joy?
- Do you view service as something you do every once in a while, or is it a lifestyle?
- Do you see yourself as a servant of God? Do you take joy in being his servant?

For Further Reading

Romans 12

Reason #5

TO ESTABLISH
PEACE ON EARTH

You might find it difficult to read the opening lyrics to one of the most well-known Christmas carols without singing the tune:

> *Hark! the herald angels sing,*
> *Glory to the newborn King!*
> *Peace on earth and mercy mild,*
> *God and sinners reconciled!*

These lines summarize Luke 2:13-14. In those verses, the author Luke recalls a prophecy from the book of Isaiah, who predicted that Jesus would be the "Prince of Peace," among other things (Isaiah 9:6). So I wonder: If Jesus is the Prince of Peace and he wants us to have peace, why do we see so little peace in the world? Although it is not my intention to fully answer this question here, I will give a couple of general causes for the lack of peace in our world.

Reason #1: People cannot get along due to selfishness and pride. Every person is unique, having their own specific desires and wants. When we put our own wants above others, problems arise (James 4:1-2). Additionally, it makes us feel good when we see ourselves as better than other people. Individuals in one group share characteristics with one another while individuals in another group share other characteristics; sometimes those groups focus on their differences and, in pride, feel "better than" others. This leads to arguing, strife, conflict, and even war. It has been said that we often ask God why there is so much suffering in the world, but the reality is that God should be asking us that question instead. Our own failures and mistakes certainly suggest that we're wrong to point the finger at God and blame him for the problems of the world.

In Christ, there is no room for holding grudges against others or wanting to harm them. One beauty of Christianity is that no one is superior, no one is privileged. Many who lived in the ancient Roman empire found the Church attractive for this very reason. It consisted of all different kinds of people who supposedly hated each other, yet through Christ, they lived in harmony and love. In Christ, two opposite groups can become one together in unity and purpose: the walls of hostility and divisions between them are totally destroyed and broken down by Jesus, who is our peace (Ephesians 2:14).

Reason #2: Only those who accept the peace that Jesus gives can experience true inner peace. Consider the following verses in which Jesus is talking to his disciples:

"Peace I leave with you; my peace I give you. I do not give to you as the world gives. Do not let your hearts be troubled and do not be afraid" (John 14:27).

"I have told you these things, so that in me you may have peace. In this world you will have trouble. But take heart! I have overcome the world" (John 16:33).

In these verses we see that Jesus bestows peace upon those who follow him, but that does not necessarily ensure freedom from all troubles. In fact, as long as there is sin in this world, there will be trouble and a lack of peace. But if your life is marked by a constant lack of inner peace, you are probably chasing after and opening the "gifts" that the world has to offer. Seeking things that this world defines as successful will not lead to peace. Accept instead the gift that Jesus gives, remembering that he is a very different kind of gift-giver. Because Jesus is the ultimate giver of life and peace, those that reject him will not be able to experience the peace that he intends to give.

Reason #3: The plans of the Prince of Peace have not yet fully been accomplished. Just as the Old Testament gave us previews of the New Covenant, of Jesus' birth, the Bible also gives us previews of a paradise that is to come. One day, when Jesus does away with all evil and ushers his people into heaven, there will be no more sin and then we will finally experience a world characterized by peace. What will that look like? Returning to the prophet Isaiah, we can see one of the grandest visions of the future:

The wolf will live with the lamb,
 the leopard will lie down with the goat,
the calf and the lion and the yearling together;
 and a little child will lead them.
The cow will feed with the bear,
 their young will lie down together,
 and the lion will eat straw like the ox.
The infant will play near the cobra's den,
 and the young child will put its hand into the
viper's nest.
They will neither harm nor destroy
 on all my holy mountain,

for the earth will be filled with the knowledge of
the Lord
   as the waters cover the sea. (Isaiah 11:6-9)

Scholars debate whether Isaiah refers to a time when this will be fulfilled on this earth or if we will see this only in the new heavens and new earth, but one thing is sure: there will be a time when God puts an end to all strife. As we rest in the promises of Jesus and in his provision for all things both now and in the future, we can enjoy true peace. So "Let the peace of Christ rule in your hearts" (Colossians 3:15).

Questions to Consider
- Is your life marked by peace? When people enter your home, do they get a picture of what the Prince of Peace looks like? How or how not?
- Is there anything you need to do to experience the peace that only Jesus gives? Why or why not?

For Further Reading
Psalm 32

Reason #6

TO TRAIN
MEN

What was Jesus' number one focus throughout his three-year ministry?

To perform miracles?

To preach on the Kingdom of God?

Something else?

I would argue that the number one focus was not on his miraculous interactions with individuals nor with the masses. Neither was it about any specific pithy statements, teaching points, or sermons. It was to train up men who would later change the world.

Not long after Jesus met the disciples, he announced to them their new profession: to be fishers of men. But he knew that they would not be successful in their careers if they did not have the proper training. Can you think of any profession that does not require training? In order to be successful in their ministry, the disciples were helpless and in need of some serious training.

Jesus was to the disciples a walking, living seminary. Everything Jesus did and said was done for them to grow and learn.

Frequently in the Gospels we see Jesus relating to a specific person (such as the woman at the well, Zacchaeus, etc.), but let us not forget that the disciples were there, watching and learning how Jesus ministered to others. The things that they needed to learn could not be imparted overnight. They needed to know how to teach, how to face adversity, how to pray, how to listen to the Spirit. Most of all they needed to be convinced of what God's kingdom was all about and that Jesus was Lord of all. One of my favorite authors, Christopher J. H. Wright puts it this way:

> [The disciples] were to be with him. That is, they would simply spend time with Jesus, learning from him, being trained by him, understanding his identity and mission, bearing the cost of radical discipleship, witnessing his life and teaching, his death, and above all his resurrection. This in itself made this group of twelve so unique, so much so that when Judas dropped out, the criteria they set for whoever should replace him included the same elements – he had to have been a witness of Jesus from the days of John the Baptist to the resurrection.[3]

Jesus knew that it would take three years of training. There are no short cuts or crash courses when it comes to preparing oneself to be useful in God's kingdom. We live in an age where when we want something, we want it NOW. I am often encouraged when I hear young people say they want to be great for God. This is a good desire, but if it is not matched with the willingness to spend time preparing, then their reach is often limited.

The training that Jesus gave was not just information, it was about transformation too. Take a look at this passage from John 13:12-14:

When he had finished washing their feet, he put on his clothes and returned to his place. "Do you understand what I have done for you?" he asked them. "You call me 'Teacher' and 'Lord,' and rightly so, for that is what I am. Now that I, your Lord and Teacher, have washed your feet, you also should wash one another's feet. I have set you an example that you should do as I have done for you."

We see here that Jesus did not want his disciples to learn facts about serving, he wanted them to be transformed into servants. Information is one thing, doing is another. Doing is just what the disciples did when Jesus left them with the command: "Go and make disciples of all nations."

Without the disciples, Christianity would have been a short-lived movement. The Gospels came about through the disciples' writings, new churches were formed based on the disciples' teachings, new areas were brought hope through the disciples' preaching and travelling, and many became convinced of Christianity as they witnessed the disciples dying as martyrs. I do not deny that it was God's power working through them to do those things, but it was them carrying out those actions.

Above, I mentioned the disciples were called to be fishers of men. In Acts, right before Jesus departed earth, he told his disciples they were to be witnesses, they were to testify of him. Isn't it interesting that Jesus' first and last words to his disciples included giving them a job description? As we have seen, when he called them, he told them they were to be fishers of men and when he left them, he told them to be witnesses for him. This was more than a job with a list of tasks. No, he was defining what their very purpose and identity was to be.

Questions to Consider

- Would you describe yourself as a fisher of men? A witness to Jesus?
- If you have a heart to do great things for God, are you willing to prepare?
- Who are you learning from? Who is learning from you?

For Further Reading

John 15

Reason #7

TO TEACH US
TO PRAY

Most of us as children grow up participating in an activity or hobby. It might be art, dance, music, sports, etc. Mine was sports. There were lots of kids in my neighborhood and I was always outside catching a baseball, throwing a football, or kicking a soccer ball around. I even participated in some teams and leagues and had coaches help show me how to be a better player. So, regarding football, I knew how to throw the ball, whether it be a short pass or a long one that needed to be lofted over a defender.

Now let's imagine for a moment and suppose the following happened: What if, when I was little, I saw Peyton Manning (or insert the name of who you think is the best quarterback of all time) walking down the sidewalk while I was out with my friends playing football? What would we do? We would probably at first shout for joy and want an autograph or a selfie; but if he was willing to hang around for a while longer, what do you think we would do?

Yes, exactly, we would ask him to show us how to throw a football. We would want to learn from THE expert!

This is how it is with Jesus when he taught the disciples and others how to pray. It was not like people couldn't pray or knew nothing about prayer before Jesus came around. Many excellent prayers are recorded in the Bible before Jesus came onto the scene. The disciples realized that they had the expert on prayer with them, so they asked him how to pray. They wanted to learn from the best. They could and did pray, but they wanted to do it even better. When Jesus was asked to give a lesson on prayer, he recited what is known as "the Lord's Prayer." It is found in Matthew chapter 6 and Luke chapter 11.

I think that if Peyton Manning had a few minutes to teach me about throwing a football, he would probably give me some tips and pointers to keep in mind as I practiced throwing in the future. He would spare me of all the minute details that I would probably soon forget anyways or would perhaps just cause confusion or information overload.

This is true of the Lord's Prayer. I don't think Jesus gives us a word-for-word "perfect prayer." We also can be sure that Jesus did not intend to give an exhaustive teaching about prayer. Instead, I think his goal for the Prayer was to impart some principles to keep in mind as we practice the discipline of prayer, as we talk to God himself.

Let's look at a few of these principles:

1. To pray well, you need to know who you are talking to.

Jesus starts out saying "Our Father in heaven, hollowed be your name." The word "heaven" includes the expanse of the whole universe and the word "hallowed" simply means totally pure and separate. So, when we pray, we are praying to a spiritual being who is so vast and powerful even the universe cannot contain him and he is so pure and distinct from us. Good prayers start with a correct attitude of humility before God, recognizing him for who he is.

2. When praying, submit to God and what he is doing and trying to accomplish.

Jesus goes on to say "Your kingdom come, on earth as it is in heaven." This phrase means that we understand that God has an agenda, and it is not that we come to God in prayer demanding that he fulfill our own agenda. We submit to his plan and agree that we are agents of his kingdom.

In a great book that I have read about prayer, *Praying with Paul: a Call to Spiritual Reformation*, D.A. Carson says this:

> Brothers and sisters in Christ, at the heart of all our praying must be a biblical vision. That vision embraces who God is, what he has done, who we are, where we are going, what we must value and cherish. That vision drives us toward increasing conformity with Jesus, toward lives lived in the light of eternity, toward hearty echoing of the church's ongoing cry, "Even so, come, Lord Jesus!" That vision must shape our prayers, so that the things that most concern us in prayer are those that concern the heart of God. Then we will persevere in our praying, until we reach the goal God himself has set for us.[4]

3. It's ok to ask for God to supply our needs.

Jesus continues the prayer "Give us this day our daily bread." We have physical, emotional, and spiritual needs and God knows about them before we ask. Thus, it is only natural that we ask God, because when asking we are acknowledging the fact that all of our necessities are truly given by him. Consider again the following words from D.A. Carson's book mentioned above: "There is more to praying than asking, but any sustained prayer to the God of the Bible will certainly include asking."[5]

4. Our prayers should also focus on our sanctification.

The prayer concludes: "And forgive us our debts, as we also have forgiven our debtors. And lead us not into temptation, but deliver us from evil." Here, Jesus emphasizes our walk with God in obedience to him. We realize that we are to conduct ourselves "in manner worthy of the gospel of Christ" (Philippians 1:27). We recognize that God guides us in our struggle against sin and that God forgives us when we make mistakes. And we rejoice in the fact that we can live distinctly on earth. We can show others what a godly life looks like, but God knows that we struggle with this often. As Christ has shown, why not turn to God and ask him for help in our daily battles and shortcomings?

Before closing, I would like to mention a few other points on prayer that we learn from other biblical passages:

- We must plan to pray. (Mark 1:35)
- We should pray for others, even our enemies. (Matthew 5:44)
- There is power in prayer. (Mark 9:29)

Questions to Consider

- How can you implement some of these tips into your prayer life?
- Can you think of any other passages that further teach us on prayer?

For Further Reading

Psalm 86

An excellent book on prayer is *Praying with Paul* by D.A. Carson.

Reason #8

GIVE CLARITY
ON RELIGION

The temple was a place that was hugely important in the day-to-day cultural and religious life of the Jewish people. Thus, one of the most tragic events in all of Judaism was when the temple was destroyed in roughly 586 BC as a result of the Babylonians attacking and invading Jerusalem. This tragedy caused a number of shifts in how the Jews practiced their religion. As the temple was the place where sacrifices were made, they were no longer carried out. Over time, there was a gradual increase in energy and zeal towards studying and applying the Law as best they could.

Even though the temple was rebuilt in 515 BC, the gradual rise in placing more and more emphasis on the Law continued. According to scholar J. Julius Scott, there was an "increased focus upon the meaning of the law for daily life . . . The general term most frequently used to describe the result is 'legalism.' Legalism itself is a broad category, a general way of thinking, that is popularly defined as 'strict, literal conformity to a legal or religious code.'"[6]

Bruce Metzger defines legalism as "that concept of religion

31

which makes religion consist in conformity to the Law, and promises God's grace only to doers of the Law."[7] Indeed, the majority of scholars agree that during the time between the Old and New Testaments (roughly 400 BC to 0), as well as during Jesus' day, Rabbinic Judaism was legalistic at its core, they were seeking to gain salvation and favor from God by meticulous observation of the law.

Different groups within Judaism came about as people differed in their view of how exactly the Law was to be interpreted and applied. We see Jesus interacting with the different groups in the New Testament, some of which are:

The Scribes: professional interpreters of the law who applied the law to various legal situations in the daily affairs of the Jews.

The Pharisees: the largest religious group within Judaism. The historian Josephus wrote that the Pharisees had many additional teachings apart from their Law recorded in the Bible. Both the scribes and pharisees were called "hypocrites" by Jesus.

The Sadducees: This group was made up of the social elite and had a major influence on the temple rituals and political affairs of the state of Israel. They adhered to a strict reading of the Jewish written Law, whereas the Pharisees placed more emphasis on the oral traditions of the Law.

The Essenes: This group is not mentioned in the Bible, but historical evidence shows that that their views of the Law caused them to practice voluntary poverty and asceticism (separating oneself from the world and seeking to avoid all forms of pleasure).

Many in these distinct groups earned their status in the community by their ability to show to what extent they were willing to obey the Law. In general, their motives were purely out of selfishness than anything else. They cared more for the letter of the Law than the heart of the Law. They believed they were better than others who were not like them.

There were others who were not in any of these sects, they were affiliated to no particular "flavor" of Judaism. It is easy for us to imagine that these people would be very confused as to how exactly they should follow out the Law. They were also probably humiliated at times by those "religious" people who said they were better than the rest.

Jesus' came to put an end to this kind of thinking and teaching. The various sects had been around long enough and had beaten people up with rules for too long. It was time for a new teaching to arrive. A teaching that would get back to the heart of the issue. Establishing a religion based on following rules was not a way to get closer to God or win his favor, on the contrary, it led people further away from him.

In the words of pastor Todd Wagner, Jesus came to remind everyone that "God's Word is not full of God's rules; it is full of His love and plan to rescue, redeem, and reengage with us."[8]

Jesus was very much appalled that the so-called "religious" leaders were leading everyone astray with a religion based on rules. Indeed, his harshest words were reserved for these groups of people. In Matthew 3:7 he calls the Pharisees and Sadducees a "brood of vipers." Later in chapter 23, we see Jesus repeatedly call them hypocrites. Look at his words for them in 23:27-28:

> Woe to you, teachers of the law and Pharisees, you hypocrites! You are like whitewashed tombs, which look beautiful on the outside but on the inside are full of the bones of the dead and everything unclean. In the same way, on the outside you appear to people as righteous but on the inside you are full of hypocrisy and wickedness.

Jesus was so upset because God is opposed to the prideful ones. We do not have anything to be prideful of when it comes to earning God's love. We all are loved by God the same and we all do not deserve the measure to which he loves us.

The Titanic crashed some 400 miles away from shore. With the icy temperatures, people died of hypothermia in just minutes of time. Imagine if you were one of the ones who did not get onto a life raft and found yourself trying to swim in freezing waters amongst the wreckage. Now think about how silly and prideful it would be if you said to someone else who was not as great a swimmer as you were: "Ha ha! you're never gonna make it to shore! Look at me and my swim skills! Yours are nothing compared to mine!" That would be so foolish because even if you were a better swimmer, your swimming skills were not going to get you out of the situation. Perhaps you could have made it 100, 1,000, or even 10,000 feet further to shore than the others, but your fate was the same: ending up dead in the sea.

Jesus came to show that obeying rules to earn something does not work because no one is perfect. We all fall short of the glory of God. We cannot win our way to heaven by obeying rules more than someone else. He came to put an end to the thinking and teaching of the Pharisees. Unfortunately, 2,000 years later, many still think that religion is about having an outward appearance or by following certain rules.

Questions to Consider

- In what ways is my thinking like that of the Pharisees?
- Can I do anything to earn my way to heaven?
- Am I a better person than others if I have found religion?

For Further Reading

Galatians 2:16-21

If you want to go even deeper on this subject, I highly recommend the book *How Good is Good Enough?* by Andy Stanley.

Reason #9

TO RESIST TEMPTATION

In Reason #2, I discussed how Jesus came to live out a perfect life. He obeyed the Law perfectly, something that no human being was able to do or is able to do. He was one with the Father and he knew that his purpose was to live out a perfect life in order to be a perfect sacrifice.

The Gospels of Matthew, Mark, and Luke all tell of a time when Jesus was tempted in a special way, and these passages have become known as "The temptation of Christ." I think this title is a little bit misleading, as surely Jesus faced many temptations all throughout his life. It was not like this was the only point in time that he was tempted or needed to overcome temptation. Nonetheless, it would be good for us to take into account a few observations regarding the time when Christ was in the desert and tempted by the devil.

As you may recall, Jesus was tempted by Satan three times. He tried to entice Jesus to 1) turn stones into bread, 2) have God rescue him miraculously after jumping off a high ledge, and 3) rule over all of the world's great kingdoms and thus receive earthly fame and honor.

1 John 2:16 states: "For everything in the world—the lust of the flesh, the lust of the eyes, and the pride of life—comes not from the Father but from the world." It is clear that the devil wanted to tempt Jesus on all three of these levels.

Thomas Aquinas, one of the most influential theologians in history, expounded on the temptation of Christ in his monumental work, *Summa Theologiae*. In section 3, he states that it was totally fitting and right that Jesus was tempted.[9]

He quotes Hebrews 14:15 a couple of times, which says "For we do not have a high priest who is unable to empathize with our weaknesses, but we have one who has been tempted in every way, just as we are—yet he did not sin."

Gregory the Great, (who became pope in 590) stated: "It was not unworthy of our Redeemer to wish to be tempted, who came also to be slain; in order that by his temptations he might conquer our temptations just as by his death he overcame our death."[10]

Returning to Thomas Aquinas, he points out that some people may come to believe that if a person is holy enough, then they will be free from temptations. Aquinas refutes this, stating that no person may consider themselves so great as to be free from experiencing temptation because Christ, the perfect holy man, suffered through temptation.

Regarding the temptation of Christ, many have also observed a juxtaposition between Christ's victory over temptation and Adam's fall and defeat when confronted with temptation. Adam lived in a perfect garden, he was at one with the presence of God and had everything he needed around him, yet he failed. He disobeyed God having all the resources available to help him remain faithful. Jesus, on the other hand, was tempted in the harshest of conditions—in the middle of a desert and after 40 days of fasting—yet he did not give into temptation! Paul contrasts Adam and Christ in Romans chapter 5, verse 19: "For just as through the disobedience of the one man [Adam] the many were made sinners, so also through the obedience of the one man [Jesus] the many will be made righteous"

Now as I stated above, we know that Jesus was surely tempted in many ways throughout his life besides the moment in the desert. As a boy he was not immune from the temptations of other boys living in the neighborhood.

During his ministry, surely he was tempted to punch his opponents who were trying to trick him, defame him, and even kill him.

He was probably tempted to fight or perhaps to run and hide when Judas came with the Roman guards to arrest him. Instead of escaping conflict, fighting against the Romans, or even simply yelling out names against them, he healed the ear of one of the guards. The ear happened to be cut off by Peter, who, opposite of Jesus, gave into his temptations and sought to seek his own vengeance. He let his own emotions and desires dictate what was right at the moment.

We have such a wonderful example in Jesus. But he does not just leave us with a good example, he knows that we need supernatural help in order to overcome evil. For this reason, he gives us the Holy Spirit, who empowers us to experience victory and can even change our hearts and desires to be more in tune with God's will. Thanks be to God that he knows our fight against temptations!

Questions to Consider

- How can you, like Jesus, be more connected to God and understand more about your mission and purpose for your life? (both of these aided Jesus in his fight over temptation)
- Does it help to know someone else has gone through the same trials that you have experienced in the past or are going through now?

For Further Reading

James 1:12-18

Reason #10

TO CONDEMN
FALSE TEACHERS

If you grew up in the 1980's like I did, you are probably familiar with the movie *The Karate Kid*. In one of the scenes the
hero of the story, Daniel, is being chased down by his enemies.
He tries to run and escape, but as he tries to leap over a fence, he
is caught and dragged down. Some begin to kick and beat him
while others stand around taunting and laughing. He is hurt
and has already been defeated, but his enemies want to do even
more damage. The leader says that they must give a severe punishment and show no mercy on him. One of them helps hold
Daniel up while the other one attempts to do a running kick to
give a final destructive blow. Out of the blue, Daniel's mentor
Mr. Miyagi jumps over the fence and protects Daniel, blocking
the kick just in time. Daniel's enemies then seek to take on Mr.
Miyagi in a fight, but they are all defeated, as Mr. Miyagi proves
to be too skilled for them.

Now this is not the best analogy, but at least it gives us
somewhat of an idea of what it was like when Jesus came on the
scene. The common Jews had suffered more than enough years
of beatings by false teachers. Jesus came on to the scene just in

time. The so-called "religious" leaders of the day were not just burdening other people with rules to follow, they were actually leading them further away from what it means to know God and follow him. Jesus was sick and tired of this and came to clearly speak out against false teaching.

Consider the words of Jesus in Matthew 18:6-7:

> If anyone causes one of these little ones—those who believe in me—to stumble, it would be better for them to have a large millstone hung around their neck and to be drowned in the depths of the sea. Woe to the world because of the things that cause people to stumble! Such things must come, but woe to the person through whom they come!

And in Matthew 7:15:

> Watch out for false prophets. They come to you in sheep's clothing, but inwardly they are ferocious wolves.

And then there is the scene in Jerusalem just days before Jesus' death:

> On reaching Jerusalem, Jesus entered the temple courts and began driving out those who were buying and selling there. He overturned the tables of the money changers and the benches of those selling doves, and would not allow anyone to carry merchandise through the temple courts. And as he taught them, he said, "Is it not written: 'My house will be called a house of prayer for all nations'? But you have made it 'a den of robbers.'"
>
> The chief priests and the teachers of the law heard this and began looking for a way to kill him, for they feared him, because the whole crowd was amazed at his teaching. (Mark 11:15-18)

I believe there are a couple of reasons why the crowds were amazed at his teaching. The first has to do with the content of his teaching. It was from the very heart of God, so people recognized it as being authoritative and true. The second reason they were amazed was from the method of his teaching. No one had stood up against the false teachers in a way that he had. Certainly, others had recognized that what was going on in the temple was wrong, but they had not been as bold against evil as Jesus had.

The disciples, who carried out the ministry of Jesus, had to continue the "fight" against false teachers. It is a theme that comes up frequently in Acts and the New Testament letters, so I will just mention a couple of instances here.

Galatians 1:7-9:

Evidently some people are throwing you into confusion and are trying to pervert the gospel of Christ. But even if we or an angel from heaven should preach a gospel other than the one we preached to you, let them be under God's curse! As we have already said, so now I say again: If anybody is preaching to you a gospel other than what you accepted, let them be under God's curse!

And 2 Peter 2:1-3:

But there were also false prophets among the people, just as there will be false teachers among you. They will secretly introduce destructive heresies, even denying the sovereign Lord who bought them—bringing swift destruction on themselves. Many will follow their depraved conduct and will bring the way of truth into disrepute. In their greed these teachers will exploit you with fabricated stories. Their condemnation has long been hanging over them, and their destruction has not been sleeping.

Sadly, there are still many around today who use "religion" as a means for gaining wealth, power, and fame at the expense of others. This should not be surprising as they have been around throughout the centuries.

We may never cross paths with these religious leaders, but in our everyday lives we still may have opportunities to stand up for the truth. With our mouths we may correct, teach, and rebuke someone with the truth of Scripture. With our lives we may obey God even when it is difficult.

Lord, may we be lights of truth which stand out against a dark world!

Questions to Consider

- When was the last time you had the opportunity to speak out against false claims?
- Why is it important for us to take a firm stand for truth?

For Further Reading

Psalm 1

Reason #11

TO FURTHER THE HOLY SPIRIT'S WORK

There are many instances we see the Holy Spirit at work in the Old Testament. Right at the beginning of the Bible, we see that the Holy Spirit was involved in the creation of the universe:

> In the beginning God created the heavens and the earth. Now the earth was formless and empty, darkness was over the surface of the deep, and the Spirit of God was hovering over the waters. (Genesis 1:1-2)

The Spirit is also given credit in the work of creation in Job 33:4 and Psalm 104:30.

Other ways we see the Spirit at work in the Old Testament are to:

Skill people for specific tasks:

> Then the Lord said to Moses, "See, I have chosen Bezalel son of Uri, the son of Hur, of the tribe of Judah, and I have filled him with the Spirit of God, with wisdom, with understanding, with knowledge and with all kinds

of skills— to make artistic designs for work in gold, silver and bronze, to cut and set stones, to work in wood, and to engage in all kinds of crafts. (Exodus 31:1-5)

Grant supernatural wisdom and understanding:

So Pharaoh asked them, "Can we find anyone like this man, one in whom is the spirit of God?" Then Pharaoh said to Joseph, "Since God has made all this known to you, there is no one so discerning and wise as you. You shall be in charge of my palace, and all my people are to submit to your orders. Only with respect to the throne will I be greater than you." (Genesis 41:38-40)

Enable Prophesying:

So Saul went to Naioth at Ramah. But the Spirit of God came even on him, and he walked along prophesying until he came to Naioth. (1 Samuel 19:23)

Give special strength for war:

The Spirit of the Lord came on him [Othniel], so that he became Israel's judge and went to war. The Lord gave Cushan-Rishathaim king of Aram into the hands of Othniel, who overpowered him. (Judges 3:10)

Even though the Holy Spirit was definitely at work in the times of the Old Testament, we know that the full scope of the ministry of the Holy Spirit would not be fulfilled until after Jesus returned to heaven. In an earlier entry we discussed how the covenants of the Old Testament were good, but the greatest covenant of all was the New Covenant established by Jesus. In the Old Testament God's character of grace can definitely be seen, but it is in Jesus Christ that we see God's grace on full display and highlighted with a spotlight. In the same way, the Holy Spirit was definitely at work during Old Testament times, but it is through Jesus that the Holy Spirit is able to fully shine.

Jesus understood how essential the ministry of the Holy Spirit would become, proving to be beneficial in giving glory to God as well as in the lives of those in whom the Spirit would dwell. Indeed, Jesus makes a profound statement to his disciples in John 16:7, telling them that it was better for them to have the Holy Spirit than to have Jesus with them. In the words of pastor J.D. Greear: "Having the Holy Spirit *in* them, he said, would be better than having his bodily presence *beside* them."[11]

This is why the day of Pentecost was such an important event in history. It marked the beginning of a new era, an era in which the Holy Spirit's very presence would dwell in the souls of men and women. Consider these two verses regarding this point:

> "Now it is God who makes both us and you stand firm in Christ. He anointed us, set his seal of ownership on us, and put his Spirit in our hearts as a deposit, guaranteeing what is to come." (2 Corinthians 1:21-22)

> "Do you not know that your bodies are temples of the Holy Spirit, who is in you, whom you have received from God?" (1 Corinthians 6:19)

The very fact that we can have God's Spirit living within us should cause us to marvel at his excellence! Jesus has been called Emmanuel, which is God with us. But with the Holy Spirit, we have God in us! "Wonder of all wonders, the same Spirit who empowered Jesus's earthly life and sacrificial death now has been given to us today. He not only works on us, and through us, but *he dwells in us*."[12]

Yet the Holy Spirit does not dwell in everyone on the planet. Not everyone has been forgiven of their sins through faith in Christ. God, and thus the Holy Spirit, is perfect and cannot dwell in places that are unholy and unclean. Our hearts must be washed and cleaned before the Holy Spirit can come in. The Holy Spirit himself even takes on a vital role in the work of cleaning us, in our salvation. He convicts us our sin and enables us to understand what Jesus did for us. One of my favorite passages in all of Scripture is Titus 3:4-7. I encourage you to read it slowly and pause a minute to reflect on what it means:

> But when the kindness and love of God our Savior appeared, he saved us, not because of righteous things we had done, but because of his mercy. He saved us through the washing of rebirth and renewal by the Holy Spirit, whom he poured out on us generously through Jesus Christ our Savior, so that, having been justified by his grace, we might become heirs having the hope of eternal life.

What a wonderful passage! The most important role of the Holy Spirit is to point us towards the one who can save us, the one who was born miraculously 2,000 years ago.

In closing, there are so many other ways the Holy Spirit ministers to us and through us for the building up of his church, but to touch on them all would make this post into a book, which is longer than what is intended here. But the principle work that the Holy Spirit does is convict people of their state of being guilty before God, enabling them to come into relationship with him.

Questions to Consider

- Do you view the Holy Spirit as a person or as a force?
- How can you pray more to the Holy Spirit?
- How can the Holy Spirit point you more towards Jesus?
- How can the Holy Spirit enable you to talk to others about God or build up God's church?

For Further Reading

Galatians 5:16-26

Reason #12

TO BREAK
THE SILENCE

The time between the last events of the Old Testament and the first ones in the New Testament covers a span of roughly 400 years. At the end of the Old Testament, we see the people of Israel trying to piece their society back together after returning from exile. Moving to the New Testament we find a very different setting: the Jews are under the rule of the Romans, several different sects within the Jewish community are on the scene, and we see the synagogues as a place of meeting for religious purposes. Indeed, for us today it seems that the separation between the books of Malachi and Matthew is only one flip of a page, yet we often forget just how long 400 years is and everything that happened in that time gap.

The time between the Testaments is sometimes referred to as the "period of silence" or "years of silence." These terms are used because there were no special messengers of God who proved to be prophets, nor were there biblical books being written during this time. So it could be said that God was silent as for over 400 years he did not speak through spokesmen nor have specific revelation to be recorded as Scripture.

On the historical scene, however, we can say that the years between the Testaments was anything but silent.

As far as wars are concerned, perhaps there is no other span of time that compares to what took place between 400 BC to 0. Take a look at some of the wars that happened:

410-340 Second Sicilian War
400-387 Persian -Spartan War
395-386 Corinthian War
382-379 Olynthian-Spartan War
379-371 Theban-Spartan War
370-350 Satrap's Revolt
355-346 Third Sacred War
340-338 Latin War
327-304 Second Samnite Wars
322-320 First Diadoch War
319-316 Second Diadoch War
315-311 Third Diadoch War
315-307 Third Sicilian War
307-301 Fourth Diadoch War
306-303 Seleucus I Nicator's invasion of India

This list only contains the wars during the 4th century BC, and it is not even an exhaustive list, it only includes some of the major ones! Power struggles all throughout the Intertestamental period (a fancy term for the time between the Old and New Testaments) saw the end of many major world empires: The Greeks, Egyptians, Carthaginians, Seleucids, Macedonians, and Persians. Mankind was definitely marked by a heightened longing for power, fame, and comfort during this age of time.

Another way that people were "flexing their muscles" was in the intellectual arena. Socrates, Epicurus, Plato, Zeno of Citium (founder of Stoicism), and Aristotle all lived during this time and obviously had a huge impact on the development of many different fields in philosophy. If you happen to be a teacher of Geometry you can thank Euclid for having a job. He was the founder of this branch of mathematics, and lived in 300 BC Archimedes was another brilliant mind to make a mark during the Intertestamental period, he was a mathematician and is known to be the first person to calculate the value of pi.

In spite of the world's quest for increased intelligence, power, and fame, there was still strife in the world and there was a lack of peace. The Jews had gone astray in their religious practice. They were tired of the revolving door of empires which conquered them. The nations were at war. An established language (Koine Greek), and the building of a network of roads had both connected the world together like no time before. The time had finally come for God to break the silence and come on to the scene once again. The time was perfect for a miracle baby.

The first story of a baby being born in the New Testament is actually not Jesus, but rather his cousin, John the Baptist. His parents were Zachariah and Elizabeth. Zachariah's name means "God remembers" and Elizabeth's name means "God of oath." John's name means "God is a gracious giver." What an interesting way to break the silence from the Old Testament! God remembers that he is a God of covenant who keeps his promises and that he is a gracious giver!

John the Baptist served as the last prophet before Christ and his purpose was to tell people that God was going to do something entirely unique through his cousin Jesus. His birth was just a small prelude to what would be the real start of the New Testament: the birth of Jesus Christ. John the Baptist was a wakeup call, to get people ready for the miracle baby. Jesus was born at just the right time as all of God's plans are always on time.

This reminds me of an earlier point in history when God also came on the scene miraculously to begin the story of redemption, it occurs in Genesis chapter 12. From Genesis 3-11 we basically see what happens to mankind when we are left on our own. This was a time of progress for humans, yet as far is morality is concerned it was marked by a downward spiral of destruction. Suddenly, out of the blue, God calls upon Abraham and tells him that he has something special planned in order to allow humans to come out of their dreary situation. God was going to do something special with not just the family of Abraham, but with all of the world's nations. Indeed, God's redemption of mankind was being put into place.

Regarding God's plans breaking through the silence and calling Abraham, Christopher J. H. Wright, in *The Mission of God's People* writes:

> The greatest human civilizations cannot solve the deepest human problems. God's mission of blessing the nations has to be a radical new start. It requires a break, a radical departure from the story so far, not merely an evolutionary development from it.[13]

In our times today, it may appear that God is silent, which has led many to question whether God is really at work in this world. Again, we find ourselves surrounded by a quest for power, knowledge, and money. Combat and war are common stories in our newspapers. not to mention war. To this God says:

> *Let not the wise boast of their wisdom*
> *or the strong boast of their strength*
> *or the rich boast of their riches,*
> *but let the one who boasts boast about this:*
> *that they have the understanding to know me,*

that I am the Lord, who exercises kindness,
   justice and righteousness on earth,
   for in these I delight. (Jeremiah 9:23-24)

Do you know this God that came to earth as a human?

He may seem silent now, but he is at work and can be heard and known by reading the Bible.

He will once again show up miraculously and all eyes will be on him once again.

Questions to Consider

- Do you see God as completely in control of human history?
- In what other ways did God use the events of the time between the Testaments to prepare the scene for the birth of Jesus?

For Further Reading

Luke 1

Reason #13

TO BECOME
SIN

As mere humans, we wrestle with many mysteries regarding our God. There are no answers which fully explain some of the mysteries which we are faced with. This should not surprise us when dealing with God our creator. For if we could fully describe him and understand him, he would no longer be deserving of our worship. Indeed, the breech between us and God is infinitely more than that which lies between us and ants.

At least for me, most of the things which leave me confounded are those that are intellectual in nature. How can we fully understand that Jesus was both God and man? The Trinity contains three persons but there is only one God, how can that be? How is it possible that God has no beginning or no end? Try to ponder on these topics for a while and you may begin to fry the electrical circuits of your brain!

Today, however, I want to touch on a mystery that perhaps is more difficult to understand ethically and morally than it is intellectually. It is one that leaves my heart restless in a way that no other mysteries do. It comes straight from the verse 2 Corinthians 5:21, which states:

God made him who had no sin to be sin for us, so that in him we might become the righteousness of God.

We know from many different passages of Scripture that Christ was a substitute for us. It was I who deserved to be nailed to a cross, for I am the guilty one who sinned against God. Many have explained Jesus being our substitute using the example of a court case scenario where someone is on trial for doing a heinous crime and found to be guilty. The judge delivers a just punishment, giving the criminal a life-long sentence in jail. However, the judge is also infinite in love, and decides that he does not want this person to suffer the time in jail, so he takes the punishment himself. In this example we have an exchange: someone who did not deserve punishment receives punishment, and someone who does deserve punishment receives none. Now this in of itself, the fact that Jesus would offer himself up as a substitute, is already an unfathomable act of love and grace.

Yet our verse in question today takes the absurdity of the cross one step even further. Taking the text at plain value, it says that Jesus *became sin.* God made him to be sin. Jesus does not simply bear the punishment for our sins—he becomes the very essence of sin.

John Gill, who was a pastor in the 18th century at a church which would later become the place where Charles Spurgeon would serve as pastor, had this to say about 2 Corinthians 5:21:

But besides all this, he was made sin itself by imputation; the sins of all his people were transferred unto him, laid upon him, and placed to his account; he sustained their persons, and bore their sins; and having them upon him, and being chargeable with, and answerable for them, he was treated by the justice of God as if he had been not only a sinner, but a mass of sin.[14]

All of the perverse acts against children. All of the hate crimes done out of prejudice. All of the brutal killings of the unfortunate. All of our small, petty sins which may not seem so harmful, but are nonetheless acts of disobedience and rebellion. Jesus did not merely die for those acts—he became those acts. There is an uneasiness about this but it is true. Jesus came to be all of that so that God in his justice could punish it and do away with it all. There are obviously no words that can make us understand this fully, perhaps it is best to just stand back in utter awe.

When we are moved emotionally to a high degree or are fully complexed by something, sometimes poetry and music explain our inner feelings best. That is why I conclude today's reading with this hymn, titled "And can it be that I should gain:"

And can it be that I should gain
An interest in the Savior's blood
Died He for me, who caused His pain
For me, who Him to death pursued?
Amazing love! How can it be
That Thou, my God, shouldst die for me?
Amazing love! How can it be
That Thou, my God, shouldst die for me?

He left His Father's throne above
So free, so infinite His grace
Emptied Himself of all but love
And bled for Adam's helpless race
'Tis mercy all, immense and free
For O my God, it found out me!
Amazing love! How can it be,
That Thou, my God, shoudlst die for me?

Long my imprisoned spirit lay,
Fast bound in sin and nature's night
Thine eye diffused a quickening ray
I woke, the dungeon flamed with light
My chains fell off, my heart was free
I rose, went forth, and followed Thee
Amazing love! How can it be
That Thou, my God shouldst die for me?

No condemnation now I dread
Jesus, and all in Him, is mine
Alive in Him, my living Head
And clothed in righteousness divine
Bold I approach the eternal throne
And claim the crown, through Christ my own
Amazing love! How can it be
That Thou my God, shouldst die for me?

Questions to Consider

- What do you think it means when it says that Jesus became sin on our behalf?

For Further Reading

2 Corinthians 5

Reason #14

TO FULFILL
PROPHECY

I believe the main point of the creation story in Genesis chapter 1 is not to give us detailed information about *how* God created the world (although certainly we can draw some conclusions as to how he did it). Nor is the author concerned so much of telling us *when* God created the world. The main point of the first chapter is to introduce us to the major subjects of the story in history: God, mankind, and the created world. Indeed, if we do not understand correctly who God is, who we are, and our role in the story and our relation to the world, then we are left confused and walking in fog.

In the first chapter of the Bible it is clear that the author wants to tell us about this great, all-powerful God. One of his defining characteristics is that his word is always true, it can be trusted all the time and is 100% effective. This is one of the most pleasant things about God. Ten times in Genesis chapter 1 we see repeated "And God said . . ." What is also repeated is "and it was so." God says something and it is done. Period.

Consider these 2 verses on God's promises:

"You know with all your heart and soul that not one of all the good promises the Lord your God gave you has failed. Every promise has been fulfilled; not one has failed" (Joshua 23:14).

"Your kingdom is an everlasting kingdom, and your dominion endures through all generations. The Lord is trustworthy in all he promises and faithful in all he does" (Psalm 145:13).

God does not just keep his word regarding future promises, he also has the power to predict the future. Throughout all of Scripture we see different prophecies made regarding specific events that would unfold in the future. Perhaps the greatest prophecies of all are those which predicted the birth and life of Jesus centuries before he was even born.

The Old Testament contains many passages which point towards Jesus, some are more direct and explicit prophecies, yet others are more subtle allusions to his life.

While people may debate over just how many prophecies there are in the Old Testament about Jesus, one thing is for sure: Jesus himself explained to two of his disciples that all sections of the Old Testament contained things pertaining to his own life: "beginning with Moses and all the Prophets, he explained to them what was said in all the Scriptures concerning himself" (Luke 24:27).

In Matthew's Gospel, it is clear that while he was putting together his book about Jesus, he identified many prophecies that were fulfilled. On 13 different occasions when writing about the life of Jesus, Matthew pauses and adds in the phrase: "this happened in order to fulfill the Old Testament prophet . . ." It was clear to him that the Old Testament Scriptures foretold some of the events that happened in Jesus' life.

Here are just a few among the many specific prophecies about Jesus that were fulfilled:

- Jesus would be a descendant of David. (2 Samuel 7:12-13)
- Jesus would be born of a virgin. (Isaiah 7:14)
- Jesus would be born in Bethlehem. (Micah 5:2)
- Jesus would minister in Galilee. (Isaiah 9:1-2)
- Jesus would be preceded by a forerunner (who was John the Baptist, Isaiah 40:3-4).
- Jesus would be despised and rejected. (Isaiah 53:3)
- Jesus would have an everlasting throne. (Daniel 7:13-14)
- Jesus would come as king riding on a donkey. (Zechariah 9:9)
- Jesus would be forsaken, he would suffer thirst, he would be scorned, and his hands and feet pierced. (Psalm 22)
- Jesus would conquer death. (Isaiah 25:7-8)
- Jesus would establish a New Covenant. (Jeremiah 31:31)

These are just a sampling and Jesus fulfilled them all. He is the only "candidate" who could fulfill every one of these prophecies! In other words, if we are to look at it purely from a mathematical standpoint, it is pretty much statistically impossible that someone else would live and fulfill all of these prophecies.

I would like to cite Walter Kaiser, one of the most prominent Old Testament scholars of our times, who has some interesting words about the connection between the Old Testament and Jesus:

As far as the case for the Messiah in the Old Testament is concerned, the relationship between the Old and New Testaments is one of strong continuity and a progressive revelation. The seminal seeds of the doctrine of the person and work of Jesus bloom and blossom in the New Testament even though the Old Testament often carried in seminal seed form much that eventually developed out of the Old. What a gracious, revealing God, and what a wonderful gift of a Savior who has come to earth once, but who is due to return once more in all his fullness and glory![15]

Jesus said that he would return once again and there are many prophecies regarding this truth. We know that God's words are always true and that what he foretells regarding future events never err. Oh, what a delight in being able to rest in the assurance of our future!

Questions to Consider

- Do you trust that God is always faithful to his word?
- Are there any promises of God that you need to cling to and trust?
- How are you doing at being faithful to your word?

For Further Reading

2 Peter 1:16-21

Knowing Jesus through the Old Testament, by Christopher J. H. Wright is one of the best books, in my opinion, on how the Old Testament points towards Christ

Reason #15

TO SHOW US
THE WAY

Often in life we come across situations where we feel like we are powerless. Think of a time (perhaps before GPS was available) when you were totally lost. You couldn't even get to a place you were familiar with, much less to where you were trying to go. This is trivial compared to other situations where we feel totally helpless. We can become confused, frustrated, or even worse, we could hurt ourselves and others if we make a wrong decision.

This is what it is like to be human. We are often confused as to our purpose, our destiny, or what we should do with our time and resources while we are alive. It is difficult to go through life without answers to essential questions. We are all "seekers" on this planet, as we try to find answers and meaning and peace.

Yet we are not left to our own on our journey. Just as the creator of an object knows best how that object should be used, God is our creator, and he knows what is best for us. He is not only our creator but he is also good, so he does not just know what is best for us, he has gone to great extent to show us what is best for our lives.

Jesus stated "If you have seen me you have seen the father (John 14:9)" And in Colossians 2:9 Paul writes: "For in Christ all the fullness of the Deity lives in bodily form." God sent Jesus to earth so we can know him and so that he could tell us what life is all about. Without Christ, we all are stuck in a dark tunnel seeking for truth, yet in him we can find truth.

Christ knew that we need help in this life. He knew that he was not just to save us and give us the possibility of living with him in heaven. No, we also need help DURING this life. It is true that Jesus said that he came to "seek and save the lost," showing us that we do need saving, but he also made statements about how he came to help us in this life. Many of these are formulated in "I AM" statements. Consider the following:

I am the light of the world. What does light do? It illuminates an area so people can see where they need to go. The full verse states "When Jesus spoke again to the people, he said, "I am the light of the world. Whoever follows me will never walk in darkness, but will have the light of life." (John 8:12). As we go through this life, if we have Jesus by our side, we never find ourselves in situations where we are totally helpless, or in complete darkness.

I am the good shepherd. Jesus uses the metaphor of a shepherd to talk about his double purpose of saving us from our sins and for guiding us in this life. He first says he lays down his life for the sheep, alluding to the fact that he would become the true sacrificial lamb to be offered up for us. Then he says that he provides the sheep (us) with pasture (John 10:9) and that he intends to give us life to the full (John 10:10).

I am the bread of life. Bread was a staple of the diet for those living in the ancient Roman world. So, when saying he is our bread, Jesus is saying that he sustains us in this life. We are to go to him continually in order to receive what we need spiritually to live lives that would glorify God.

I am the way, the truth, and the life. Jesus does not point us in a certain direction, towards truth and to life, he IS life! The context of this statement in John chapter 14 is how God will comfort the disciples, specifically by giving them the Holy Spirit. So again, when Jesus says he is the way, the truth, and the life, he is talking both about his ability to provide a way for us to get to heaven, and also that he provides a way for us to live on earth.

Questions to Consider

- How is Jesus making a difference in my life today? Is my faith in God and Jesus something that just affects my future?
- What do I need to give over to Jesus today in order to obey him and trust him?

For Further Reading

Psalm 25

Reason #16

TO CLAIM
THE THRONE

The event which is simply known as "The Triumphal Entry" is a significant one in the life of Jesus. It is recorded in all four of the Gospels (Matthew 21:1-11, Mark 11:1-11, Luke 19:28-44, John 12:12-19). Jesus' Triumphal entry is celebrated on Palm Sunday, which many of you may know is observed exactly one week before Easter Sunday. In order to reflect on this event and draw some conclusions, it is fitting that we understand the context and background.

Jesus had been in the public ministry for three years or so. Through his teachings, powers, and interactions with the public, his fame had spread more and more. The hatred in the hearts of those who opposed him had also increased all the more. At first, they grumbled and argued with him. Over time they became jealous, which then grew into full-blown hate. They had already looked for ways to kill him, but now they were going to have him killed—no matter what measure needed to be taken. They simply could not stand that someone else had more authority and more fame then they had.

Jesus had turned water into wine and had provided enough

food for over 5,000 people with just a few loaves of bread and fish, but now, right before Palm Sunday he was to perform his most spectacular miracle up to this point: Raise a person from the dead. His friend Lazarus had died, and he wanted to bring him back to life, not just for Lazarus' sake, but also in order for his disciples to believe in him all the more (see John 11:15). As they were in the wilderness, the disciples clearly thought it was a completely crazy idea to even think about going to Bethany, which was just outside of Jerusalem, for they knew that it meant danger. When Jesus said he was going, they replied "But Rabbi, a short while ago the Jews there tried to stone you, and yet you are going back?" (John 11:8). Yet he did go and he did raise Lazarus from the dead. The results of this event are probably what you expect: Jesus was THE talk of the town, he was on the lips and in the minds of everyone, not just a few followers or his opponents.

Perhaps the best way to describe the situation right before the Triumphal entry is in John's gospel, where chapter 11 concludes:

> When it was almost time for the Jewish Passover, many went up from the country to Jerusalem for their ceremonial cleansing before the Passover. They kept looking for Jesus, and as they stood in the temple courts they asked one another, "What do you think? Isn't he coming to the festival at all?" But the chief priests and the Pharisees had given orders that anyone who found out where Jesus was should report it so that they might arrest him. (John 11:55-57)

It was not just any time, it was the time for Passover, the largest religious ceremony of the year. Jerusalem was teeming with people who had flocked there in order to participate in this mandatory festival. His close followers and allies, others that were merely curious about him, and his haters were all awaiting his arrival. He was to go to Jerusalem, but the way he did it and how the people received him was what made this event special.

We know that Jesus was in Bethany, which was just about two miles east of Jerusalem, with the Mount of Olives lying in between. He asked his disciples to find him a specific donkey and bring it to him, which he rode along the way as he entered Jerusalem. Jesus had walked thousands of kilometers throughout his life, travelling many times back and forth from the area of Galilee to Jerusalem. He certainly didn't need to ride a donkey these last few kilometers, so why did he do so at this particular time?

First of all, common folks mainly walked to get around, but throughout the history of Israel it was kings who were known to use mules or donkeys (2 Samuel 13:29, 1 Kings 1:33). Secondly, according to Matthew's Gospel, "it was to fulfill what was spoken through the prophet: 'Say to Daughter Zion, See, your king comes to you, gentle and riding on a donkey, and on a colt, the foal of a donkey'" (Matthew 21:4-5, quoting Zachariah 9:9).

Regarding how the crowds received him, they received him like a king! They spread forth palm branches before him and threw their cloaks on the ground before him. They were shouting:

"Hosanna!"
"Blessed is he who comes in the name of the Lord!"
"Blessed is the king of Israel!" (John 12:13)

They were quoting from Psalm 118. That particular Psalm was part of a group of Psalms known as the "Hallel," which consists of Psalms 113-118. They were often cited during important Jewish festivals, and it very well may have been these Psalms that Jesus sang with his disciples at the Passover meal in the upper room just a few days after the Triumphal Entry. The theme of Psalm 118 is about God's power to save and conquer. The Jews knew their Bible and knew that a descendant of David was going to come as king to rescue them. They knew many Psalms pointed toward events in the future and attributed this Psalm to Jesus. On Psalm 118, Charles Spurgeon states: "That the Psalmist had a prophetic view of our Lord Jesus is very manifest; the frequent quotations from this song in the New Testament prove this beyond all questions."[16]

The only thing is that the Jews were expecting a political king who would rescue them from the Roman rule. They had been conquered by the Romans in 63 BC and had hopes for a physical savior. Here, finally in their midst was their coming king in the capitol city. They rejoiced over the fact that finally they would be freed from all those who oppressed them. Yet Jesus did not overthrow the Roman rule and free the Jewish people from their control. As a result, the crowds no longer followed him. Just a few days after the Triumphal Entry, the crowds were now shouting to have him executed. Only a small group of individuals understood that he was king in a different way.

> The kingdom of God which he preached and inaugurated was not an earthly, political kingdom, but the rule of God in the hearts of people who know and serve him. But this was not the kingdom which the people expected or wanted, and so they rejected Jesus as their Lord.[17]

Jesus does not fulfill our expectations all the time, but that does not mean he is not our King.

In conclusion, I will cite Charles Spurgeon again, who talks of the fact that there is a second Triumphal Entry that will occur sometime in the future:

We know who it is that cometh in the name of the Lord beyond all others. In the Psalmist's days he was The Coming One, and he is still The Coming One, though he hath already come. We are ready with our hosannas both for his first and second advent; our inmost souls thankfully adore and bless him and upon his head unspeakable joys.[18]

Questions to Consider

- Do you view Jesus as your spiritual King? Are you a member of his kingdom?
- Do you seek to serve the king? Do you serve him with joy?
- How do you handle it when the King does not fulfill your expectations? Do you abandon him like the crowds?

For Further Reading

Psalm 96

Reason #17

TO GAIN VICTORY
OVER DEATH

As many of us recall, there was only one thing that God prohibited Adam from doing in the garden of Eden: eat of the tree of the knowledge of good and evil. Indeed, God said "for when you eat of it you will certainly die." (Genesis 2:17). Adam knew the consequence would be tragic, but I am sure he was also a little bit uncertain of what exactly God meant. For a brief period of history our human race lived free from the consequences of death and had no full knowledge of what it meant to die. It was a foreign concept.

When Adam and Eve sinned, they were given the punishment that God warned of: death. (Remember, in Reason #14 we saw that God is always true to his word.) It was the most tragic event in all of human history, and for this reason it is often referred to simply as "The Fall." It is impossible for us to fully understand what happened to us at The Fall, but we are not totally ignorant on the subject, for the uneasiness of death, the reality of death, and the sadness of death constantly remind us that all is not totally fine and dandy and the world is not as it should be.

From Adam's time and forward, to use the words of Paul, "death reigned" (Romans 5:14, 17). Now what does this mean that "death reigned?" And what exactly is death?

To answer the first question, the fact that death reigns means that we have no power over it. There is no solution for it and there is no way to escape it. It is a fact of the matter, a consequence of our disobedience.

The second question requires a little bit more space to answer. I believe there are several different dimensions or ways in which we experience death.

Firstly, death is physical. Our bodies decay and we know that one day our physical bodies will die. We will say a final good-bye to everyone we know, whether that be when our body experiences death or theirs. Additionally, we suffer the consequences of living in an environment that itself is broken and under a curse.

Secondly, death is spiritual. Spiritual death is simply being isolated, estranged, and distanced from God, who is the very giver of all life and all things good. In the state we are in when we come into this world, we cannot enjoy his presence among us because we are spiritually dead. Consider the evidence of what happened when Adam and Eve sinned: they hid from God, were ashamed and felt guilty, were afraid, and were kicked out of the garden, for God could not dwell with sinful men. Our spiritual death leads to the third and fourth dimensions:

Thirdly, death is intellectual. Our minds are not capable of being fixed solely on the things of God. We have warped thinking. We constantly try to rationalize or give excuses for bad behavior. We see this in Adam as he pointed his finger at both Eve and God, saying that it was their fault and he had nothing to do with it.

Fourthly, death is social. Read the Genesis story a little

longer and you will find all accounts of social evil: lying, jealousy, murder, etc. If you don't recall the stories of sin in the book of Genesis, simply open your daily newspaper and you will see that socially we are a mess. Christopher J. H. Wright describes the social dimension of death this way: "every human relationship is fractured and disrupted – sexual, parental, familial, societal, ethnic, international – and the effect is consolidated horizontally through the permeation of all human cultures, and vertically by the accumulation throughout the generations of history."[19]

Now time for the good news: Jesus came to put death to death. He knows that we have no way to defeat death so he defeated it for us! Although we still sin and thus must experience physical death, death is no longer our end and it is no longer victorious over us! Additionally, we may be freed from the spiritual, intellectual, and social dimensions of death. When we believe on Christ, his Spirit enters us and enables us to live a new life.

Consider Romans 8:11: "And if the Spirit of him who raised Jesus from the dead is living in you, he who raised Christ from the dead will also give life to your mortal bodies because of his Spirit who lives in you."

Jesus' enemies sought out to get rid of him once and for all. They had him killed, yet having him killed was at the same time the act that brought about Jesus' ultimate victory over them.

Athanasius is one of my favorite theologians and he is considered to be one of the greatest theologians all time. I tried to get my wife to consider the name Athanasius for our son, but that thought didn't last long. At any rate, I conclude with some precious words of Athanasius regarding Jesus' victory over death:

> He, the Life of all, our Lord and Savior, did not arrange
> the manner of his own death lest He should seem to be

afraid of some other kind. No. He accepted and bore upon the cross a death inflicted by others, and those others His special enemies, a death which to them was supremely terrible and by no means to be faced; and He did this in order that, by destroying even this death, He might Himself be believed to be the Life, and the power of death be recognized as finally annulled. A marvelous and mighty paradox has thus occurred, for the death which they thought to inflict on Him as dishonor and disgrace has become the glorious monument to death's defeat.

You know how it is when some great king enters a large city and dwells in one of its houses; because of his dwelling in that single house, the whole city is honored, and enemies and robbers cease to molest it. Even so is it with the King of all; He has come into our country and dwelt in one body amidst the many, and in consequence the designs of the enemy against mankind have been foiled and the corruption of death, which formerly held them in its power, has simply ceased to be. For the human race would have perished utterly had not the Lord and Savior of all the Son of God, come among us to put an end to death.[20]

Questions to Consider

- How sure are you that Jesus has given you victory over death?
- How does victory over death affect the way you live today?

For Further Reading

John 11

Reason #18

TO RISE FROM
THE GRAVE

My stepdad told me an interesting story the other day. He worked many years in various hospitals. One day he was catching a ride in an elevator along with a doctor. He asked the doctor "Have you saved any lives or cured any diseases today?" The doctor's response: "No, all I have done is prolong death."

Previously, we saw that man has a serious problem called death, yet Jesus conquered it. Today's discussion is really just a continuation or natural outflowing of Jesus' victory over death, for the way in which Jesus proved his victory was to rise from the dead.

You may recall that Lazarus was another guy that was able to come back to life after being dead several days. Yet there are two major differences between Lazarus' resurrection and Jesus': 1) Lazarus eventually died again, and 2) Lazarus did not resurrect himself on his own power. The fact that Jesus had the power to save himself and that his tomb is the only empty tomb on earth proves that he is God and has ultimate authority over all things, even death!

After he arose from the dead, he had a new body, a glorified one. He appeared to the disciples and others and then shortly after ascended directly into heaven. From that day on, he has been in the business of changing lives, even though he cannot be seen physically.

Athanasius points out keenly that Jesus' ability to work in the hearts of people proves that he is still alive:

> Dead men cannot take effective action; their power of influence on others lasts only till the grave. Deeds and actions that energize others belong only to the living. Well, then, look at the facts in this case. The Savior is working mightily among men, every day He is invisibly persuading numbers of people all over the world, both within and beyond the Greek-speaking world, to accept His faith and be obedient to His teaching. Can anyone, in face of this, still doubt that He has risen and lives, or rather that He is Himself the Life? Does a dead man prick the consciences of men?[21]

Jesus, who was the first among the resurrected, serves as an ultimate source of hope for those that believe in him. Paul, in Philippians 3:20 states that "our citizenship is in heaven. And we eagerly await a Savior from there, the Lord Jesus Christ, who, by the power that enables him to bring everything under his control, will transform our lowly bodies so that they will be like his glorious body."

Two key observations regarding this passage are: 1) That God will resurrect our bodies, and 2) Our bodies will be different in the resurrected state.

Paul again gives us assurance of being resurrected in 1 Corinthians 6:14: "By his power God raised the Lord from the dead, and he will raise us also."

The resurrection did not come cheap, it came at the expense of Jesus' death. In other words, there would have been no resurrection without Jesus first living an obedient life as a human and then suffering for us. Being resurrected and obtaining a place in heaven is not for everyone. Those that "bear the cross" of Jesus will be those who are resurrected with him. Many people want to receive the benefits of heaven without being a disciple of Jesus, but there are no short-cuts.

There are some who deny the resurrection of Christ all together. Perhaps they do this because they know that if the resurrection did happen, then Christianity must be true. Dr. Gary Habermas, a leading apologist, has written a great deal on the evidence for the resurrection of Jesus. He gives a list of 12 historical facts surrounding the resurrection of Jesus that even skeptical scholars adhere to, the 12 facts include:

1. Jesus died by Roman crucifixion.
2. He was buried, most likely in a private tomb.
3. Soon afterwards the disciples were discouraged, bereaved and despondent, having lost hope.
4. Jesus' tomb was found empty very soon after his interment.
5. The disciples had experiences that they believed were the actual appearances of the risen Christ.
6. Due to these experiences, the disciples' lives were thoroughly transformed. They were even willing to die for their belief.
7. The proclamation of the Resurrection took place very early, from the beginning of church history.
8. The disciples' public testimony and preaching of the Resurrection took place in the city of Jerusalem, where Jesus had been crucified and buried shortly before.
9. The gospel message centered on the preaching of the death and resurrection of Jesus.

10. Sunday was the primary day of worshiping and gathering.
11. James, the brother of Jesus and a skeptic before this time, became a follower of Jesus when he believed he also saw the risen Jesus.
12. Just a few years later, Paul became a believer, due to an experience that he also believed was an appearance of the risen Jesus.[22]

Point number six is in my opinion a very powerful point. All of the disciples were not just *willing to die* for their belief that Jesus arose again, but the great majority of them *did die* in a gruesome manner at the hands of their opponents. It is a fact that some people may risk their lives for something they believe is true but in reality is not true. However, it is not logical for people to die for something they know did not happen. The disciples knew first hand if Jesus had risen from the dead or not. If they knew he had not resurrected from the dead, they would not have risked their lives to the point of torture and death, they would not have suffered all that for what they knew was not true. Yet the reality is that they did know Jesus rose from the grave and therefore they were willing to die for this truth.

Even though these points of argument and others may help you believe that the resurrection is true, that is not my main goal here. I don't want to defend the resurrection over celebrating the resurrection. It is to be celebrated like nothing before or after.

There are many songs which celebrate our risen Lord, one of my favorites is "In Christ Alone." The lyrics are as follows:

In Christ alone, my hope is found
He is my light, my strength, my song
This cornerstone, this solid ground,
Firm through the fiercest drought and storm.

What heights of love, what depths of peace,
When fears are stilled, when strivings cease!
My comforter, my all in all
Here in the love of Christ I stand.

In Christ alone, Who took on flesh,
Fullness of God in helpless babe!
This gift of love and righteousness,
Scorned by the ones He came to save.
'Til on that cross as Jesus died,
The wrath of God was satisfied
For ev'ry sin on Him was laid
Here in the death of Christ I live.

There in the ground His body lay,
Light of the world by darkness slain
Then bursting forth in glorious day,
Up from the grave He rose again!
And as He stands in victory,
Sin's curse has lost its grip on me
For I am His and He is mine
Bought with the precious blood of Christ.

No guilt in life, no fear in death
This is the pow'r of Christ in me
From life's first cry to final breath,
Jesus commands my destiny.
No pow'r of hell, no scheme of man,
Can ever pluck me from His hand
'Til He returns or calls me home
Here in the pow'r of Christ I'll stand.

Questions to Consider

- Are you sure that you will be resurrected? How can you be sure?
- What "costs" are you paying now as a follower of Christ?

For Further Reading

1 Corinthians 15

I invite you to celebrate by listening and/or singing along with a recorded version of the song "In Christ Alone." You will find numerous to choose from. Two of my favorites are by Lauren Daigle and a recording from the Together for the Gospel Conference by Sovereign Grace Music.

Reason #19

BECAUSE HE
LOVES US SO

Being a husband and a father, I have come to learn some things about love. Most of them are probably things I should have learned earlier in life, but often I don't learn anything I am supposed to until I am in a situation where I have to. I definitely have lots more to learn as well. Anyways, one of the things I have come to realize is just to what lengths love compels us to sacrifice our own wants in exchange for putting the needs of others first. All of you husbands, wives, fathers, and mothers reading this think: taking care of sicknesses in the wee hours of the night, dropping or changing plans in a heartbeat to attend to a special need, shelling out significant amounts of cash and resources on things that we typically wouldn't spend on, etc. This shouldn't come as too much of a surprise, as we learn from the famous chapter on love in 1 Corinthians that love is not self-seeking and it always protects.

As Christians, we know intellectually that we are supposed to love everyone, not just our close friends and family. Because of this, others should see us sacrificing our time and energy in order to serve them. However, we know from experience that we are much more prone to make great sacrifices for those that are most dear to us. I don't want to debate whether or not there are different "degrees" of love, but my conclusion based on observation is that the more I treasure someone, the more likely it is that I will do loving acts for them. I don't think that is necessarily a bad thing, it just shows we are not capable of loving everyone in the same way. Our love is limited in scope.

Our love is not just limited in scope, it is also limited in its consistency. It is impossible for us to love at all times, as we often make selfish decisions which are not the best for others. If you think I am wrong, just try this experiment: pick just one person in the entire world and commit yourself to loving them perfectly. Whether it be your friend, neighbor, spouse, child, or parent, eventually you will fail. Our love is not perfect because we ourselves are not perfect.

But God's love is perfect. It has no beginning and has no end. It is not limited in scope, for it reaches out to everyone, to every being, and to all of his creation. It is a tragedy when someone thinks that God does not love them, or that he loves someone else more. He loves us and desperately seeks to do things on our behalf. Remember, love is not self-seeking and it always protects. God seeks us where we are and he wants to protect us: not just from others, not just from future perils, but also from our own vile ways. He loves all people, and his love is shown to be clearly in a class of its own as it even extends towards those who are his enemies. Romans 5:8 says "God demonstrates his own love for us in this: While we were still sinners, Christ died for us." He chose to seek our benefit and get rid of the breech between us and him, even though it is ourselves that are at fault.

> "For God so loved *the world* that he gave his one and only Son, that whoever believes in him shall not perish, but have eternal life." (John 3:16, emphasis added)

In the Psalms, the adjective which is most often used to describe God's love is "unfailing." Consider just two examples:

"But I trust in your unfailing love; my heart rejoices in your salvation" (Psalm 13:5).

"Satisfy us in the morning with your unfailing love, that we may sing for joy and be glad all our days" (Psalm 90:14).

The Hebrew word that has been translated as "unfailing" is also sometimes translated as "great," "faithful," "good," "kind," and "merciful." Our God is great, faithful, good, kind and merciful; thus, his love is as well.

God's love is not just limitless in scope, it is also not limited in its consistency. From our viewpoint, love is something like a switch that can be turned on and off. Sometimes our love switch is on and we love others well, while other times the switch is off and we fail to love others well. It is not like that for God, it is not something that he turns on and off. Love is not something that God DOES, it is what he IS. God is love. He cannot not love as that would contradict his very nature. He cannot love more, nor can he love less. In fact, his love is infinite because he himself is infinite.

David and other writers of the Psalms understood the magnificence of God's love, yet they were not even around to witness God's most clear act of love towards mankind: sending his only son on our behalf. He did this because love goes to extreme measures to take care of and provide for others. In other words, even though we cannot fathom such love which gave up so much, we should not be surprised, because that is the essence of what love itself is all about.

One of the loftiest pursuits one can take part in during this life is to try to understand how great God's love is. Paul, in Ephesians 3:17-18, writes: "And I pray that you, being rooted and established in love, may have power, together with all the Lord's holy people, to grasp how wide and long and high and deep is the love of Christ." One of the best ways to start out on this pursuit is to think about Christ's life and how it is a reflection of God's love. Is it possible to think about Christmas without thinking about God's love?

As we come to know God and understand the sacrifice of love that he gave for us on our behalf, we are then called to show others who God is by loving others. If we fail to love others, we fail to be Christ-like.

Practically every letter written in the New Testament has parts which encourage us to excel all the more in the quality of love: As Christians we are called to "be devoted to one another in love" (Romans 12:10), "do everything in love" (1 Corinthians 16:14), "show [others] the proof of your love" (2 Corinthians 8:24), "serve one another in love" (Galatians 5:13), "bear with one another in love" (Ephesians 4:2), "make my joy complete by being like-minded, having the same love" (Philippians 2:2), "and over all these virtues put on love" (Colossians 3:14), "may the Lord direct your hearts in God's love" (2 Thessalonians 3:5), "set an example for the believers in speech, in conduct, in love, in faith and in purity" (1 Timothy 4:12), "pursue righteousness, faith, love and peace" (2 Timothy 2:22).

Thank you, God, for the great love you have shown us in going to extreme measures to seek our good. You came to earth motivated by love.

"Greater love has no one than this: to lay down one's live for one's friends." (John 15:13)

Questions to Consider

- How do I relate with others? Is my motive out of love or are there underlying selfish motives?
- When I am at a large gathering of people I don't know, do I seek out a specific type of person (ethnicity, socio-economic status, age, etc.?)
- In what ways can I grow in my understanding of God's love?
- How sure am I that God loves me?

For Further Reading

1 Corinthians 13

Listen to or read the lyrics of the hymn "How Deep the Father's Love for Us." One version by Sovereign Grace Music here: https://www.youtube.com/watch?v=cUpZ-USm-Fw

Reason #20

TO RESCUE US

When I was in the Boy Scouts, I spent a full week at summer camp learning how to be a lifeguard. I began swimming at a young age and had always been comfortable in the water. But learning how to deal with and save another person who was drowning proved to be far from easy. The class was over 30 years ago, but I still remember it for all the interesting information as well as it being physically challenging. We learned that for a lifeguard, jumping into the water to save a drowning person is always the last option to take—it should only be done when no other option is available. This is why you will normally see different things around pools for lifeguards to use such as long poles with a hook-like loop at the end, rescue tubes, life rings, etc. I remember being taught that if we were at a place where no tools were available, we were to be resourceful and use whatever we had on hand to try to reach the victim who is drowning, even to use things like the very jeans we were wearing, which could be used to reach out to the victim and pull them in. Why is jumping in the water and directly swimming up to the one who is drowning the last resort? Well, a drowning person is a force to be reckoned with. They are usually in a panic, flailing their arms around looking to grab on to anything they can and they are not in a place where they can reason well. Even the most skilled, strong swimmers can easily be grabbed and pulled under water and even die from others who are drowning themselves. It is risky business and this is why a lifeguard's job is so noble.

Switching our conversation to spiritual things, I would argue that Jesus Christ is the most noble of all lifeguards. Just as a lifeguard usually sits atop a platform so as to see all the swimmers, Christ, before he was born, was in a perfect place of glory and love, together with the Father and the Holy Spirit. Yet he saw our condition and recognized that we could not save ourselves.

John, in his story about Jesus says this about him:

> In the beginning was the Word, and the Word was with God, and the Word was God. He was with God in the beginning. The Word became flesh and made his dwelling among us. We have seen his glory, the glory of the one and only Son, who came from the Father, full of grace and truth. (1:1-2,14)

It is important to remember that Jesus existed before he was born on this earth. Jesus became flesh, he was willing to leave heaven and face the dangers and perils of this world. He was willing to risk everything in order to perform the most fabulous rescue of all!

There is no partiality with God, he demands the same thing from everyone: perfect righteousness. Because no one is perfectly righteous, we all find ourselves in the same situation: drowning and in need of rescue. That's the bad news. The good news is that God supplies what he demands. The giving of his only Son was a great sacrifice but it was the only way for us to be rescued, the only way we could be given life. If we, out of our own strengths and abilities, were able to save ourselves, then he would not have needed to rescue us. Indeed, no lifeguard would jump in to save another if the other person was capable of making it to shore on their own.

Consider Ephesians 2:1-5:

> As for you, you were dead in your transgressions and sins, in which you used to live when you followed the ways of this world and of the ruler of the kingdom of the air, the spirit who is now at work in those who are disobedient. All of us also lived among them at one time, gratifying the cravings of our flesh and following its desires and thoughts. Like the rest, we were by nature deserving of wrath. But because of his great love for us, God, who is rich in mercy, made us alive with Christ even when we were dead in transgressions—it is by grace you have been saved.

Before we are saved by Jesus, the Bible says we are "dead." It says this because without Jesus in our lives we are separated from God and are slaves to sin—our sin controls us. Another reason why it says we are dead is because a dead person can do nothing to change their situation—we are totally powerless to save ourselves. Paul also talks about our ability [or lack thereof] to save ourselves in Galatians 2:21: "if righteousness could be gained through the law [obeying rules], Christ died for nothing!"

If I was ever drowning in the sea and rescued by a lifeguard, I know there is one thing I would do the rest of my life: look for ways to thank him/her and honor him/her. This is how those who have been rescued by Jesus seek to live their lives: in gratitude for what he has done and wanting to do everything possible to honor him.

Perhaps if you feel like you have never been saved and given life by Jesus, you can admit your situation to him. Admit that you have sinned and are not perfectly righteous and accept his provision as a Savior.

The words of this song that my daughter learned at VBS this past year may be fitting for your prayer:

Lord, here I am. And the waves are crashing all around. I need you God and I need you now!
Rescue me, I can feel the water rising. Rescue me, Jesus.
Rescue me, Lord I'm in so deep and I feel powerless to save myself, only you can be the help I need. Rescue me.
Rescue me. Jesus, rescue me.[23]

A prayer that is something along those lines may be the kind of prayer you need to pray today. I would also add that it would be good to declare to him what you need rescuing from. There may be many things going on in your life that make you feel like you are drowning, but the biggest reason of all and the most that you need God to save you from is your own sin.

Questions to Consider

- Do I feel like I have been rescued by Jesus, or am I drowning in the sea of life?
- Do I understand what Jesus rescues me from?
- Am I living a life of gratitude to Jesus for what he did to me?

For Further Reading

Philippians 2:5-11

Reason #21

TO DISPLAY
GOD'S POWER

Near the conclusion of John's book that he wrote about Jesus, he gives his readers an insight into the purpose he had in writing it:

> Jesus performed many other signs in the presence of his disciples, which are not recorded in this book. But these are written that you may believe that Jesus is the Messiah, the Son of God, and that by believing you may have life in his name. (20:30-31)

It is clear that John wanted whoever happened to get their hands on his book to believe in Jesus. Actually, not just believe in Jesus but believe that he was the Messiah (the coming king that the Old Testament spoke of) and the Son of God. He does not want his readers to conclude that Jesus was merely a good person or an excellent teacher. Nor does he want them to think that Jesus was a great prophet or someone that established a new religion.

John, in spending three full years with Jesus, had come to this conclusion about who Jesus was. He saw that knowing Jesus and who he was changes everything. Upon believing, one experiences a new kind of life.

Clearly John had a lot of material to choose from when it came time for him to put down on paper what he wanted to say about Jesus. He chose to include only a handful of Jesus' miracles. Let's take a brief look at some of the signs:

Turning Water into Wine (John 2:1-11): Jesus does not just turn water into wine, it is great wine. This proved that Jesus had power over creation. He has the ability to make new things and to make things qualitatively better.

Destruction and restoration of Jesus' body (John 2:13-25): During a time when there was much activity and movement at the temple in Jerusalem, Jesus shows his anger over the fact that it had become a place of corruption whereas it was intended to be a place where people connected with God. Jesus then predicts that his body (which he also calls "temple") would be destroyed, but that it would be repaired and restored in three days' time. His prediction of his own resurrection shows that Jesus has power over time.

Healing the Nobleman's Son (John 4:46-54): A man holding a high political office has a son who is sick and about to die. He departs his town and heads out to where Jesus is and asks him to please come to his town in order to heal his son. Jesus did not go see the boy, he declared him healed right there on the spot. This shows that Jesus has power over space.

Healing the Lame Man (John 5:1-15): Jesus encounters a man who had been paralyzed and unable to walk for 38 years. Jesus simply says to the man "pick up your mat and walk" and he immediately was able to walk again! In this miracle, Jesus shows his ability to heal life-long uncurable diseases. He also shows there is power in his words.

Feeding the Multitude (John 6:1-15): This is a well-known miracle where a large crowd had gathered to listen to

Jesus' teachings, but they found themselves in a tough spot as they were all hungry and too far from town to walk back before it was dark. With a couple of fish and loaves of bread, the entire crowd—at least 5,000 in number—were fed, and there was a lot left over as well. Similar to the water into wine miracle, here we see that Jesus has power over creation. In the former one the emphasis was on Jesus' power to alter the quality of things, yet here we see an emphasis on Jesus' power to alter the quantity of things.

Raising Lazarus (John 11:1-44): Jesus receives news that his friend Lazarus had died. Arriving to the town where Lazarus lived, Jesus receives news that he had been buried four days before. Jesus then raises Lazarus from the dead. This showed that Jesus has power over death and life. Of course we know that Jesus again showed this power by raising himself from the dead.

There are other miracles recorded in the book of John as well as in the other Gospels. Simply taking into account the ones mentioned here, we see that Jesus has power over creation, time, space, death, life, and disease!

It is interesting that John uses the word "sign" to describe each of the miraculous acts of Jesus and not "miracle." To John, the miracles were not just mere tricks or displays of power for the purpose of show. They were signs that pointed to something. Signs that served as a signal showing that Jesus was truly God.

But miracles are not the only "signs" used by John to show that Jesus was all that he said he was. Sometimes specific individuals, through their words and actions, served as signs. At the beginning of his gospel he presents John the Baptist. Verses 29-30 of chapter one state:

> The next day John saw Jesus coming toward him and said, "Look, the Lamb of God, who takes away the sin of the world! This is the one I meant when I said, 'A

man who comes after me has surpassed me because he was before me.'"

John the Baptist was himself merely a sign that was used to point others towards Jesus Christ. His purpose was not to bring attention to himself, he wanted to put the spotlight on the King who had come from heaven.

We too, are to be "signs" and Jesus himself said that others would come to know about God according to how we speak and act here on earth.

Questions to Consider

- Do I believe that Jesus had power to perform miracles?
- How can I be a sign which points others towards Jesus?

For Further Reading

Psalm 66

Reason #22

TO HEAL OUR DISEASES

Praise the Lord, my soul;
*   all my inmost being, praise his holy name.*
Praise the Lord, my soul,
*   and forget not all his benefits—*
who forgives all your sins
*   and heals all your diseases,*
who redeems your life from the pit
*   and crowns you with love and compassion,*
who satisfies your desires with good things
*   so that your youth is renewed like the eagle's.*

This is how my favorite Psalm (103) in the Scriptures starts out. David is thinking about what God does. What does he do? Look at the verbs in this Psalm to find the answer: he forgives, he heals, he redeems, he crowns, and he satisfies! Certainly he does a lot more, but just thinking about those alone cause David to want to do nothing else but praise God. Understanding the right things about God helps us to have the right attitude and puts our lives into the right perspective.

We are all theologians. All of us have some notion about God. The question is are we going to be good theologians or bad ones? Having a true knowledge of God will give him more glory and will also mean living life with more purpose here on earth. On the other hand, having incorrect thoughts about God will only lead us astray and cause harm. Indeed, as A.W. Tozer has said, "What comes into our minds when we think about God is the most important thing about us."[24]

Unfortunately, today, many people have a skewed view on the verse I quoted above that says "God heals all your diseases." I have heard many teach that God guarantees health, wealth, and prosperity in this life. If you just have enough faith, then God will remove your problems. Or even more extreme: if you give God some money, then he will do a miracle for you. This kind of teaching is damaging as it is not just anthropocentric (human centered), it leads people to believe that they do not have a true faith in God if he does not heal them. Interpreting Scripture correctly leads us to the following conclusions:

First of all, we have no guarantee or promise of a time frame for God healing our diseases. He never promises to heal all of our diseases while we are still living on this planet. Indeed, one of the ways that he heals us of our diseases is that he allows our decaying body to perish. It is after we die that we receive new glorified bodies which cannot be afflicted with any disease.

Secondly, although not certainly the most pleasant thought, is that God sometimes actually sends or allows diseases in order to accomplish something greater in us. Scriptural basis for this can be seen in Leviticus 26:16, Deuteronomy 28:21-22, 2 Chronicles 21:18, 2 Corinthians 12:7-8, and others.

Thirdly, diseases allow us to remember that all is not right in the world; that there is evil and darkness and those things came to our creation because of disobedience. The Fall of man was catastrophic for the entire creation. Consider Paul's words in Romans 8:18-23:

> I consider that our present sufferings are not worth comparing with the glory that will be revealed in us. For the creation waits in eager expectation for the children of God to be revealed. For the creation was subjected to frustration, not by its own choice, but by the will of the one who subjected it, in hope that the creation itself will be liberated from its bondage to decay and brought into the freedom and glory of the children of God.
>
> We know that the whole creation has been groaning as in the pains of childbirth right up to the present time. Not only so, but we ourselves, who have the first-fruits of the Spirit, groan inwardly as we wait eagerly for our adoption to sonship, the redemption of our bodies.

Fourthly, our spiritual disease trumps our physical and mental illnesses. Imagine you came across a scene where a serious car accident just happened. You see one man complaining that his head hurts, yet unbeknownst to him, his leg has been severely cut and blood is squirting out all over the place. He will bleed to death if you do not quickly apply a tourniquet. Attending to the headache first would be foolish and lead to death as it would not treat the most urgent and life-threatening problem.

It is this way with our physical ailments as well. They are real and they do affect us and God does care about them, but he is infinitely more concerned with the disease which will cause us the most harm: our spiritual state of sin. When we accept Christ for who he is and what he has done for us, we are not only forgiven of our sin, but we become a new creation with "new DNA" so to speak.

Todd Wagner discusses this point, stating:

Even when Jesus was performing the miraculous, He never offered anything resembling protection from all future temptation or trouble. Nowhere in the New Testament is there an admonition to use an incantation that would free us from ever needing intercession again. Christ's interactions with people—even when He miraculously delivered or healed them—always called them to deeper dependence on Him. . . . He did not stop with concern merely for their current struggles. He knew that apart from coming to faith in Him, their coming eternal struggles were going to be infinitely worse. That is why He often followed up His care for their situational evil with a warning that they should also trust in Him as their provision for their moral evil.[25]

The disease of sin runs rampant in today's society. If we are honest, most of the affliction and strife that we see today are all brought upon by our own evil acts. I hope that as Christians we can be true agents of light in the world, carrying a message of hope and healing to a hurting world.

Questions to Consider

- Have you ever thought that if you just had enough faith then God may do some miraculous thing for you? Do you still feel that way? If not, what changed your thinking?
- Do you view your spiritual disease as far more serious and in need of healing than your physical problems?
- How can you help be an agent of God for others, a vessel used by him to bring healing?

For Further Reading

Psalm 103

Reason #23

TO BE PROPHET, PRIEST AND KING

All societies that exist, regardless of their type of government (democratic, monarchy, socialist, etc.), must have people in positions of leadership. The roles of those distinct leaders shape the very fabric which defines the society itself.

When the Israelites were rescued by God and they came out of slavery from Egypt, they were a brand-new nation which had to grow up fast regarding its political structure. Of course, God helped them in this process. He immediately gave them a Law, a set of rules and guidelines for them to live by. He also knew that they needed defined, specific roles for leaders, so he established three kinds of officials: kings, prophets, and priests.

The role of the king was to bring peace from within by establishing order amongst the Israelites, and peace from without by protecting the nation from its enemies. The king initially was God himself. Yet Israel quickly rejected God as their king. They wanted a human king like the nations around them. God gave them their desire and allowed them to appoint human kings which proved to be disastrous, indeed, the very first selected king was Saul, who did not lead the people well. Only a handful of the 42 different kings which reigned actually did good, and even those that did good had their flaws.

The role of the prophet was to be God's spokesperson before the nation. They were like messengers. When God wanted to communicate something special to his people, the prophet was to deliver the exact news that God wanted them to hear. They generally reminded the people of the covenant that they had made with God, that their continued disobedience was grounds for God to punish them.

Finally, the priests were a special group of people who were to act as a bridge between a perfect, holy God and a population which was full of imperfection. They were to maintain the relationship between God and the masses. They interceded and acted on behalf of the people before God. Amongst the priests, there was a High Priest, who was to enter the holiest place of the tabernacle once a year (the day of atonement) and confess the sins of the whole nation. Sadly, the priests became corrupt and used their role for their own gain.

In the time right before Jesus was born, Israel was in desperate need of some good leadership in its society. They had no king as they were not a free state. There were no prophets, as God had grown tired of sending his messengers over and over, only for the people to reject the message. The priests were not serving the people as they should.

This was the case for centuries. In Jewish writings between 400 BC and 0, there is much said about their longings for a glorious king, a righteous priest, and a powerful prophet.

But God had his own plan, both for Israel and all other people groups of the world. He would come as king, prophet, and priest. Jesus took on the role of all three. In fact, he not only fulfilled the three roles, he was the perfect king, prophet, and priest. He was supreme in all three compared to the other humans that assumed these roles. The kings, prophets, and priests in the Old Testament all had failed at one point or another, whereas Christ did not. Moreover, the humans holding these roles only did so for a short while, yet Christ holds these roles forever.

He is a perfect king because he has ultimate power—both from within and from without. He has power to hold his church together and bring individuals to salvation and he also has power over all our enemies. He is called King of Kings and Lord of Lords.

Secondly, in the office of prophet, Jesus is supreme because he is not just a spokesperson chosen by God, he is God himself. The words he uttered were all direct news from God. He definitely had news to tell, for he was establishing a new kind of kingdom available for all people. Similar to the prophets of old, Jesus was also for the most part rejected.

Finally, he is a perfect priest because he removes the gap between us and God. In 1 Timothy 2:5 we read: "For there is one God and one mediator between God and mankind, the man Christ Jesus." The words of 1 John 2:1 are also comforting: "My dear children, I write this to you so that you will not sin. But if anybody does sin, we have an advocate with the Father—Jesus Christ, the Righteous One." The clearest passage on Christ being a superior High Priest comes to us in Hebrews:

> Now there have been many of those priests, since death prevented them from continuing in office; but because Jesus lives forever, he has a permanent priesthood. Therefore he is able to save completely those who come to God through him, because he always lives to intercede for them.
>
> Such a high priest truly meets our need—one who is holy, blameless, pure, set apart from sinners, exalted above the heavens. Unlike the other high priests, he does

not need to offer sacrifices day after day, first for his own sins, and then for the sins of the people. He sacrificed for their sins once for all when he offered himself. For the law appoints as high priests men in all their weakness; but the oath, which came after the law, appointed the Son, who has been made perfect forever. (7:23-28)

Many theologians all throughout history have commented on Christ fulfilling these three roles (Eusebius, John Calvin, John Owen, the Roman Catholic Church, Charles Hodge, Charles Spurgeon, Lewis Sperry Chafer, and Wayne Grudem, just to name a few) You can even find an article about it on Wikipedia!

In conclusion, I leave you with the words of Charles Spurgeon:

Take Jesus in his different characters and you will see a marvelous variety—Prophet, Priest, King, Husband, Friend, Shepherd. Consider him in his life, death, resurrection, ascension, second advent; view him in his virtue, gentleness, courage, self-denial, love, faithfulness, truth, righteousness—everywhere he is a bundle of preciousness.[26]

Questions to Consider

- Consider the roles of a prophet, priest, and a king. Can you think of any more duties they had that were not mentioned in today's reading?
- How does Jesus act on your behalf as king, prophet and priest?

For Further Reading

Hebrews 5

Reason #24

TO BE OUR
REDEEMER AND
SAVIOR

Throughout this series we have been trying to answer the question: Why was Jesus born? Essentially, we are asking the same question that is on the minds of many around Christmas time: what is the real meaning of Christmas?

Christmas time can often be stressful with end of the year parties and meetings, decorations, shopping for gifts, wrapping all the gifts, etc. It is often hard to focus on the true meaning of Christmas with all the hustle and bustle. Unfortunately, I would argue that for many people the Christmas season is often just a small snapshot of what their entire life looks like. Running around from here to there, participating in activities and doing what everyone else does, yet missing out on the things of God and what he wants.

Something else that has become part of the holiday season is all the different movies and shows. My favorite is the *Charlie Brown Christmas*. As the plot develops, Charlie Brown becomes more and more frustrated and eventually shouts out to everyone:

"Isn't there anyone who knows what Christmas is all about?!" His friend Linus gives a brilliant answer.

The reason why his answer is so great is that he quotes directly from the Bible (Luke 2:8-14). God himself has told us what Christmas is all about, why Jesus was born. If we want to understand why Jesus came to earth, the best way to learn is by reading our Bibles. This is what I have tried to do with all of the reasons that we have studied so far. We have already looked at a number of passages from the Bible, let us consider a few more here.

> "For all have sinned and fall short of the glory of God, and all are justified freely by his grace through the redemption that came by Christ Jesus" (Romans 3:23-24).

> "In him we have redemption through his blood, the forgiveness of sins, in accordance with the riches of God's grace" (Ephesians 1:7).

> "He delivered us from the power of darkness and transferred us to the kingdom of the Son he loves, in whom we have redemption, the forgiveness of sins" (Colossians 1:13-14).

These passages talk about Jesus as our redeemer. Ever since The Fall, God has been involved in redeeming mankind. By far the greatest act of redemption before Jesus came on the scene was when God liberated the Israelites from the hand of the Egyptians, who used them as slaves. The Israelites were in a situation of misery and God showed up in a mighty way and rescued them. This event was so important that the Israelites held an annual festival to celebrate what God had done. It was during this exact festival that Jesus died. In Jesus we see God's ultimate act of redemption.

Jesus himself said he came to earth in order to "give his life as a ransom for many" (Matthew 20:28). The word he uses for "ransom" is the Greek word *lytron*, which is the root of the word translated as "redemption" in the three passages mentioned above.

It was used frequently for the act of liberating a slave, as one was required to make a ransom payment in exchange for the setting free of the one who was enslaved. Christ is our redeemer, he paid the price to set us free from our natural condition as sinners, as well as from the penalty to be paid for our sin. Because we are saved by the redeeming work of Christ, the terms "redemption" and "salvation" are often used with the same meaning. We have been redeemed and saved by Jesus!

Remember, it is paramount to understand what he redeemed and saved us from. If we think that Jesus is going to save us from all trouble, then we are wrong. We must understand our condition of sin and that we are guilty before him, then we can understand what he saved us from and why we need redemption.

When Jesus came, H.B. Charles notes that many people had "expectations of a coming king who would be a political champion and re-establish Israel not just as its own free state, but also re-establish its status as one of the great nations among the many in the world." They failed to recognize their biggest need and focused on something they wanted instead.

He continues:

> For God knew that what they wanted was not what they needed. It's the same in the world today. If we needed money, if that was our biggest problem, God would have sent an economist. If our biggest problem was education God would have sent a professor. If our biggest problem was government, God would have sent a politician. If our biggest problem was sickness God would have sent

a doctor. If our biggest problem was self-image God would have sent a consultant or a therapist. But our biggest problem in the world is sin so God sent a savior. We are sinners who need salvation, we cannot save ourselves but God is mighty to save.[27]

Questions to Consider

- When you want truth on a matter, do you seek to find it in God's word, or in some other outlet?
- What are opinions in the world today as to why Jesus came?

For Further Reading

John 1

Reason #25

TO GIVE GOD
ALL THE GLORY

Perhaps the most well-known of all the Christmas carols is "O Come, All Ye Faithful." One of the verses in this song states:

Sing choirs of angels
Sing in exultation
Sing all ye citizens
Of heaven above

Glory to God
All glory in the highest
O come let us adore Him
O come let us adore Him
O come let us adore Him
Christ the Lord!

The centerpiece and foundation of those words hinge on God's glory. Regarding the glory surrounding the events of Jesus' birth, another song by David Crowder Band comes to mind:

Oh, the glory of it all
Is He came here

For the rescue of us all
That we may live
For the glory of it all
Oh, the glory of it all

Oh, He is here
With redemption from the fall
That we may live
For the glory of it all
Oh, the glory of it all

The word "glory" means: 1) high renown or honor won by notable achievements, and 2) magnificence or great beauty.

Throughout this whole study we have seen Jesus' high renown. He is certainly due honor because of the many notable achievements he accomplished. He has done marvelous things and is in his very nature a thing of great magnificence and beauty. This is because he was, is, and shall always be God! God demands and deserves glory.

We have seen that Jesus rescues us from death and gives us life. He guides us towards holiness and well-being. He fulfilled all of the Old Testament prophecies—in fact, he was the Messiah that the Old Testament Scriptures point to. He is the ultimate and perfect king, prophet, and priest. You can find no one who was more noble in serving others, more authoritative in teaching on religion, more powerful in deeds and miracles performed, or more loving in sacrificing all for the benefit of others. By his Spirit, he is still busy changing lives today. Indeed, Abraham Kuyper was right when he said "There is not a square inch in the whole domain of our human existence over which Christ, who is Sovereign over all, does not cry: 'Mine!'"[28]

In our human lives, we experience and witness many things. Upon seeing an incredible physical performance in sports, eating an exceptional meal, or listening to music played by skilled hands we often describe it as being "awesome." Yet those things only inspire us for a moment. May I suggest that only God is truly awesome. For if the things in this world "wow" us, how much more should the creator of the very world cause us to stand in awe?

If you have read these 25 reasons as a way to prepare for Advent, then you are reading this entry on Christmas day. I hope that today you adore him for who he is and I hope that these studies have helped you see just how much glory and praise he deserves. If you are not reading this on Christmas day, then my hope is the same—for Christ wants you to adore him every day of your life.

All good things come to an end they say. I disagree. If it is good, let it last forever. If it is truly good, it must last forever. This book is coming to a close, but I hope that it is merely the beginning for you. You can spend your lifetime finding more reasons and understanding with more clarity why Jesus was born. Doing so will lead you to understand God himself, which will be profitable for you, both in this life and the life to come.

To conclude this book, Athanasius' words, written over 1700 years ago in his book *On the Incarnation*, are more fitting than my own:

> Such and so many are the Savior's achievements that follow from His Incarnation, that to try to number them is like gazing at the open sea and trying to count the waves. One cannot see all the waves with one's eyes, for when one tries to do so those that are following on baffle one's senses. Even so, when one wants to take in all the achievements of Christ in the body, one cannot do so, even by reckoning them up, for the things that transcend one's thought are always more than those one thinks that

one has grasped. As we cannot speak adequately about even a part of His work, therefore, it will be better for us not to speak about it as a whole. For, indeed, everything about it is marvelous, and wherever a man turns his gaze he sees the Godhead of the Word and is smitten with awe.[29]

Amen.

Soli Deo gloria.

Questions to Consider

- How have I felt more connected to God while reading this book?
- In what specific ways can I continue to celebrate Christmas and Jesus' birth in the weeks and months ahead?

For Further Reading

The story of Jesus' birth found in Luke 2

NOTES

1. Tremper Longman III and Raymond Dillard, *An Introduction to the Old Testament,* 2nd ed. (Grand Rapids, MI: Zondervan, 2006), 86.

2. John Piper, "The Sufficiency of Christ's Obedience in His Life and Death" Desiring God website, accessed May 14th, 2019. https://www.desiringgod.org/articles/the-sufficiency-of-christs-obedience-in-his-life-and-death

3. Christopher J. H. Wright, *The Mission of God's People: A Biblical Theology of the Church's Mission* (Grand Rapids, MI: Zondervan, 2010), 212.

4. D. A. Carson, *Praying with Paul: a Call to Spiritual Reformation,* 2nd ed. (Grand Rapids, MI: Baker Publishing, 2014), 43.

5. Ibid., page 14.

6. J. Julius Scott, *Jewish Backgrounds of the New Testament* (Grand Rapids, MI: Baker Books, 2000) Kindle Edition, location 1842.

7. Bruce Metzger, *The New Testament: Its Background, Growth, and Content* (Nashville, TN: Abingdon Press, 2003), 50.

8. Todd Wagner, *Come and See: Everything You Ever Wanted in the One Place You Would Never Look* (Colorado Springs, CO: David Cook, 2017), 37.

9. Thomas Aquinis, *Summa Theologiae.* Section 3 question 41. Accesed online on May 13th, 2019. http://www.newadvent.org/summa/4041.htm

10. Gregory the Great, quoted by Thomas Aquinis, *Summa Theologiae.* Section 3 question 41. Accessed online on May 13th, 2019. http://www.newadvent.org/summa/4041.htm

11. JD Greer, "What's Better Than Jesus Beside You," Desiring God website, accessed May 13th, 2019. https://www.desiringgod.org/articles/whats-better-than-jesus-beside-you

12. David Mathis, "We believe in the Holy Spirit," Desiring God, accessed May 13th, 2019. https://www.desiringgod.org/articles/we-believe-in-the-holy-spirit

13. Wright, 78.

14. John Gill, *John Gill's Exposition of the Bible*, entry for 2 Corinthians 5:21. BibleStudyTools.com website, accessed February 29th, 2020. https://www.biblestudytools.com/commentaries/gills-exposition-of-the-bible/2-corinthians-5-21.html

15. Walter Kaiser "Jesus in the Old Testament," Gordon Conwell Theological Seminary website accessed May 13th, 2019. https://www.gordonconwell.edu/resources/Jesus-in-the-Old-Testament.cfm

16. Charles Spurgeon, *Spurgeon's Classics: The Treasury of David and Morning & Evening; Daily Readings*. Charles Spurgeon and First Rate Publishers, Kindle Version, Location 98732.

17. William Lane Craig "The Triumphal Entry," Reasonable Faith website, accessed May 13th, 2019, https://www.reasonablefaith.org/writings/popular-writings/jesus-of-nazareth/the-triumphal-entry/

18. Spurgeon, Location 99178.

19. Wright, page 40.

20. Athanasius, *On the Incarnation*, Christian Classics Ethereal Library. PDF book. Chapter 4, section 24, page 19. accessed May 13th, 2019. https://www.ccel.org/ccel/athanasius/incarnation.pdf

21. Athanasius, page 23.

22 Gary R. Habermas, "Evidence for the Historical Jesus: Is the Jesus of History the Christ of Faith?" - available free of charge from www.garyhabermas.com/evidence

23. "Rescue Me" Castaway Sing & Play Music CD - Shipwrecked VBS. 2018.

24. A. W. Tozer, *Knowledge of the Holy*, Bibliotech Press, 2016. page 1.

25. Wagner, page 287.

26. Spurgeon, Location 143035.

27. HB Charles, "The Gospel and the Future of Missions," (talk given at the Southern Baptist Convention Pre-Conference on June 9, 2018 in Dallas, TX.) Video online at https://vimeo.com/277505643

28. Abraham Kuyper, Quote from Kuyper's inaugural address at the dedication of the Free University. Found in *Abraham Kuyper: A Centennial Reader*, ed. James D. Bratt (Grand Rapids, MI: Eerdmans, 1998), 488.

29. Athanasius, 43-44.

ACKNOWLEDGEMENTS

I would like to thank the wonderful local church bodies that I have been fortunate to be a part of throughout my life. All of them have shaped me as a person, formed my theology, and strengthened my Christian worldview. Though no great local church is merely a one-man effort, I would like to give special mention to the head teaching pastors: Neil Ashcraft (Scofield Memorial Bible Church, Dallas, TX), Brian Fisher (Grace Bible Church, College Station, TX), Todd Wagner (Watermark Community Church, Dallas, TX), and Sam Masters ("Centro Crecer" Baptist Bible Church, Córdoba, Argentina).

Other noteworthy influences have been guiding lights along my path. David Fulfer, a true evangelist who ignited in me a fire for evangelism. Tommy Nelson (Denton Bible Church), who is a living witness to the fact that teaching the Bible should be anything but boring. Bill Victor (Missouri Baptist Convention), my professor, mentor, and friend. Bill has a depth of theological knowledge coupled with a heart for serving others. I have been honored to work by his side on building projects for churches in Argentina as well as in training future church leaders in Latin America. Don Dinnerville, a friend who is always up for thought-provoking conversation or a fun time over a board game. Finally, my wife Sofía, along with the rest of my family who have been a constant support in all of the challenges I have taken on.